Overlooked
to
Overflow

Overlooked to Overflow

How God Elevates the Forgotten

MS. ALISHA JACKSON, MSW

Interior layout by Charlyn Samson

Overlooked to Overflow: How God Elevates the Forgotten
Written by Ms. Alisha Jackson, MSW
Cover design by Ms. Alisha Jackson, MSW
Interior layout by Charlyn Samson
ISBN: 979-8-989276868 (eBook)
ISBN: 979-8-9892768-9-9 (Paperback)
Printed in the United States of America
First Edition

For permissions, inquiries, or speaking engagements, please contact:
www.DivineWarriorLifeCoaching.com,
www.AlishaJacksonMinistries.org,
www.FaithConnectionCenter.org,
www.ABetterLifePublishingCompany.com, and/or
www.AlishaJacksonAcademy.com

Contents

Wisdom is the Beginning of Freedom

As you open these pages, know that you are taking a powerful step toward breaking free from the chains of your past, the delusions that have held you captive, and the lies that have shaped your beliefs. This moment marks the beginning of your journey toward embracing the biblical truth that will illuminate your path. The wisdom of God, rooted in His Word, is the key that will unlock your true freedom. It will guide you, heal your heart, and empower you to walk in the fullness of your identity in Christ.

By choosing to seek wisdom, you are choosing to walk in freedom—freedom from doubt, fear, and the burdens that have weighed you down. The journey ahead may not always be easy, but with each step, you will move closer to the life God has destined for you—one filled with purpose, peace, and divine wisdom that will set you free.

A Prayer for Clarity, Freedom, and Overflow

Heavenly Father,

I come before You with a heart full of faith, seeking Your wisdom and guidance. Lord, I ask that You open my eyes to see clearly the truth You have laid before me, that I may no longer be blinded by the lies of the enemy or the limitations of my past. Open my ears, Lord, that I may hear Your voice above all others, and may Your Word penetrate my heart with clarity and understanding.

I pray that You break every stronghold and bind every wicked spirit that has held me captive, whether knowingly or unknowingly. I declare freedom in the name of Jesus—freedom from the chains of fear, doubt, and oppression. Tear down every wall that has prevented me from walking fully in Your truth and purpose.

Lord, I surrender all that I am to You. Help me acquire the knowledge I need to embrace the great overflow You are pouring into my life. Teach me to receive with an open heart, to trust in Your perfect timing, and to step boldly into the abundance of Your promises.

I believe that You are a God of restoration, and I claim the victory over every obstacle that has hindered my growth. May Your wisdom guide me, Your peace fill me, and Your grace cover me. Thank You, Lord, for the overflow of blessings You are bringing into my life. I trust that You are equipping me with everything I need to fulfill Your purpose. In Jesus' mighty name, I pray.

Amen.

Dedication

To my beloved family and friends, whose unwavering faith and support have been the bedrock of my journey. This book is a testament to the power of God's love and the transformative impact of community. May it serve as a beacon of hope and encouragement to all who seek a deeper understanding of their purpose in Christ.

Preface

This book is born from a desire to equip you, the reader, with the tools and insights necessary to embark on a profound journey of self-discovery within the context of your faith. Drawing upon years of experience guiding individuals toward a fuller realization of their God-given potential, I invite you to engage with the principles outlined within these pages. Let these words serve not just as a source of information, but as a catalyst for spiritual growth and transformation. Remember, the journey to unlocking your unique gifts is a personal one, guided by the grace and unwavering love of our Heavenly Father.

Introduction

Discovering and utilizing your spiritual gifts is not merely about identifying your strengths; it's about aligning your talents with God's divine purpose for your life. This book provides a practical framework to understand the diverse ways God equips His children, encouraging you to embrace your individuality and contribute meaningfully to His kingdom. Within these chapters, you'll discover actionable steps to identify your spiritual gifts, cultivate them, and strategically deploy them for His glory. Through personal reflection, prayer, and a commitment to service, you will unlock your potential to impact the world around you, bringing hope and positive change.

Embark on this transformative journey with an open heart and a willingness to surrender to God's leading, and watch as He guides you toward a life of purpose and fulfillment.

Disclaimer

The contents of this book, *Overlooked to Overflow: How God Elevates the Forgotten*, are intended for educational, inspirational, and informational purposes only. The author is not a licensed medical or psychological professional and the information provided should not be used as a substitute for professional advice, diagnosis, or treatment. Always seek the guidance of a qualified healthcare provider or mental health professional with any questions you may have regarding your physical or emotional well-being.

The views and opinions expressed are those of the author and do not necessarily reflect the official policy or position of any affiliated organizations or institutions. The reader is solely responsible for their interpretation and application of the material presented.

Personal stories and testimonies included in this book have been shared with permission or altered to protect the privacy of individuals. Any resemblance to actual persons, living or dead, is purely coincidental unless stated otherwise.

Recognizing Your Worth

Embarking on this journey of self-discovery begins with a profound understanding: you are inherently valuable, a cherished child of God. This isn't a sentiment lightly tossed aside; it's the unshakeable bedrock upon which your entire life, your potential, your very worth rests. Before you even contemplate the lofty goals that lie ahead, before you consider the talents you might wield or the impact you might make, take a moment to internalize this truth: your worth isn't contingent upon your accomplishments, your possessions, or the opinions of others. It is intrinsic, woven into the very fabric of your being, a gift bestowed upon you by a loving Father.

This acceptance, this unwavering belief in your inherent worth, is the cornerstone of overcoming self-doubt, that insidious enemy that whispers lies of inadequacy and whispers doubt into your ear. Self-doubt is a thief, stealing your joy, your confidence, and your potential. It plants seeds of fear, choking the vibrant shoots of your God-given gifts. But you have the power to silence its deceptive voice. You can choose to embrace the truth of your immeasurable worth in Christ.

How do we begin to cultivate this profound sense of self-worth? It begins with a heartfelt recognition of God's unconditional love. Consider the parable of the prodigal son. The father's overwhelming joy at the son's return was not dependent on the son's actions or achievements; it stemmed from the unbreakable bond of love. This is the same unwavering love God has for you. Your mistakes, your failures, your shortcomings—none of these diminish His love for you. They are merely opportunities for growth, for learning, for drawing closer to Him.

To help you grasp this transformative truth, I invite you to engage in a powerful journaling exercise. Find a quiet space, a sanctuary where you can connect with God and your own heart. Take a moment to breathe deeply, centering yourself in His presence. Now, begin to list your strengths and talents. Don't hold back; let the words flow freely from your pen or keyboard. Are you a gifted musician, a compassionate listener, a skilled writer, a creative innovator? Whatever your gifts may be, acknowledge them, embrace them, and thank God for them.

As you compile this list, consider how these unique abilities might align with God's purpose for your life. Are there ways you can use these talents to serve others, to make a positive impact on the world? This isn't about seeking external validation; it's about recognizing how God has equipped you to fulfill His plan for your life. Perhaps your artistic talents can be used to inspire others, your organizational skills to serve your community, or your compassionate heart to comfort those in need. The possibilities are endless when you align your gifts with God's purpose.

This journaling exercise isn't a one-time event; it's a continuous process of self-discovery. Regularly revisit your list, adding to it as you uncover new strengths and talents. As you grow and evolve, so too will your understanding of your potential. This is a journey of unfolding, a revelation of the incredible person God created you to be.

But what about those persistent voices of self-doubt, those nagging insecurities that refuse to be silenced? It's crucial to understand that these voices are not representative of truth; they are lies whispered by the enemy, designed to keep you bound in fear and inaction. They prey on your insecurities, magnifying your weaknesses while minimizing your strengths. Recognize these lies for what they are: distortions of reality, attempts to thwart God's plan for your life.

To combat these negative thoughts, we must replace them with powerful affirmations, declarations of faith that resonate with the truth of your worth in God's eyes. Repeat these affirmations daily, speaking them aloud with conviction, allowing them to seep into your subconscious, reshaping your perception of yourself. These declarations aren't mere empty words; they are weapons of spiritual warfare, capable of dismantling the stronghold of self-doubt and releasing your God-given potential.

For instance, instead of dwelling on your perceived failures, affirm: "I am a child of God, loved unconditionally, and my worth is not determined by my accomplishments." Or, instead of focusing on your weaknesses, declare: "God has gifted me with unique talents, and I am empowered to use them for His glory." Repeat these statements, adding your own personal affirmations that speak directly to your specific insecurities and challenges. Let these words become the soundtrack of your life, constantly reminding you of your intrinsic worth and God's unwavering love.

This process of self-acceptance is not a passive one. It requires active participation, a conscious decision to embrace the truth about yourself as a beloved child of God. It involves regularly engaging with scripture, meditating on verses that speak to your worth and identity in Christ. Surround yourself with uplifting influences: Christian music, encouraging books, supportive friends and family—all these elements contribute to building a strong foundation of faith and self-belief.

Remember, your journey of self-discovery is a lifelong process, a continual unveiling of the amazing individual God created you to be. Embrace the challenges, learn from your mistakes, and never lose sight of your inherent worth in God's eyes. Your potential is limitless, your destiny glorious. Embrace the journey, trust in God's guidance, and step boldly into the future He has planned for you.

Your worth is immeasurable, your potential boundless, and your journey is just beginning. Embrace it fully, for you are uniquely and wonderfully made in His image.

The path to recognizing your worth is paved with faith, self-reflection, and an unwavering belief in God's love. It is a journey of continual growth and discovery, marked by moments of both triumph and self-doubt. But throughout it all, remember this truth: your value is not defined by your achievements but by your identity as a beloved child of God. Let this truth be your compass, guiding you toward a life of purpose, fulfillment, and boundless potential.

The journey may be challenging, but the reward is immeasurable. Embrace the journey, and watch as your God-given potential unfolds before you.

This process involves more than just acknowledging your worth; it's about actively cultivating it. It requires intentional choices, daily practices, and a willingness to challenge negative thought patterns. It's about consistently choosing to believe the truth about yourself, even when circumstances seem to contradict it. This means actively replacing negative self-talk with positive affirmations, consciously focusing on your strengths rather than your weaknesses, and celebrating your achievements, no matter how small.

Furthermore, recognizing your worth involves understanding that your value is not dependent on external validation. It's not about seeking approval from others or striving to meet their expectations.

Instead, it's about finding your identity in Christ, grounding your self-worth in His unwavering love and acceptance. This unshakeable foundation allows you to navigate the challenges and setbacks that inevitably arise in life without losing sight of your inherent value. It empowers you to persevere, to overcome obstacles, and to pursue your goals with confidence and unwavering faith.

The journey to recognizing your worth is a deeply personal one, unique to each individual. It is a process of self-discovery, a journey of uncovering the hidden treasures within your heart and soul, the gifts and talents that God has bestowed upon you. It requires self-reflection, honest self-assessment, and a willingness to confront your insecurities and fears. But the rewards are immeasurable – a life filled with purpose, fulfillment, and a profound sense of self-worth that stems from the unwavering love of God. This journey is an invitation to step into the fullness of who you were created to be, a life lived in the light of God's grace and unending love.

Finally, remember that recognizing your worth isn't a destination; it's a continuous journey. It's a daily practice of choosing faith over fear, truth over lies, and love over self-doubt. It's about cultivating a mindset of gratitude, celebrating your victories, and learning from your setbacks. It's about constantly reminding yourself that you are loved, valued, and cherished by God, and that your potential is limitless. Embrace this journey with open arms, and watch as your life is transformed by the power of God's love and the realization of your immeasurable worth. The path may be winding, but with faith as your guide, you will undoubtedly reach the destination of a life lived fully and purposefully, reflecting the glory of God.

Identifying Your Gifts

Embracing the journey of self-discovery, as we discussed, begins with acknowledging your inherent worth as a child of God. This foundation, unshakeable in its truth, empowers you to explore the remarkable potential God has placed within you. Now, let's delve into the exciting process of identifying the unique gifts and talents He has bestowed upon you – the very tools you'll use to fulfill His purpose for your life. This isn't about boasting or self-aggrandizement; it's about humbly recognizing the blessings God has given you, so you can wisely use them to serve Him and others.

The identification of your spiritual gifts isn't a solely intellectual exercise; it's a journey of the heart, guided by prayer and introspection. It's about looking beyond your perceived limitations and recognizing the seeds of potential planted within you by a loving Creator. Consider the areas of your life where you naturally excel, where tasks feel effortless and enjoyable, almost as if guided by an unseen hand. These inclinations, these innate abilities, often point towards your God-given gifts. Do you find yourself effortlessly connecting with people, offering comfort and support? This could be an indication of a gift of encouragement or pastoral care. Are you adept at organizing events, managing resources, or seeing the big picture? This might suggest gifts of administration, leadership, or prophecy – the ability to discern God's will and communicate it clearly to others.

Think back to moments where you felt truly alive, fulfilled, and deeply connected to something larger than yourself. These experiences often highlight the areas where your spiritual gifts shine brightest. Perhaps you find solace and inspiration in creative pursuits like writing, music, or visual arts. Maybe you're gifted with a sharp mind, excelling in analytical thinking, problem-solving, or teaching. These natural aptitudes aren't mere coincidences; they are manifestations of God's grace, designed to be used for His glory. Consider your passions, the activities that energize and invigorate you. Often, these passions are closely aligned with the talents God has given you.

The process of identification is deeply personal, a conversation between you and your Creator. Spend time in prayer, asking God to reveal your gifts. Don't approach this with a list of pre-conceived notions or expectations; be open to the possibility that God might surprise you with abilities you never suspected. Prayer isn't simply a request; it's a dialogue, a partnership where you invite God's wisdom and guidance into your life. Listen attentively for His quiet whispers, those subtle nudges and confirmations that affirm your path.

Reflection is another crucial element in this journey. Take time to journal your thoughts and experiences. Write about situations where you felt empowered, effective, and fulfilled. Analyze your strengths and weaknesses, not to dwell on your shortcomings but to understand your unique contributions. Ask yourself: What activities leave me feeling drained and frustrated? What tasks do I avoid, and why? Conversely, what activities leave me feeling energized and fulfilled? These reflective exercises will unveil your hidden talents and help you pinpoint your unique strengths.

Don't limit your reflection to isolated incidents. Consider patterns throughout your life. Have you consistently demonstrated particular skills or abilities across various contexts? Do friends, family, or colleagues frequently praise you for specific talents? These external validations can provide valuable insight into your God-given gifts. Listen to their feedback, but don't solely rely on their assessments. Ultimately, the final discernment rests with you, guided by the Holy Spirit.

Remember that identifying your spiritual gifts is not a one-time event; it's an ongoing process of self-discovery and growth. As you mature in your faith and experience different life challenges, new gifts and talents might emerge. Be open to the continuous unfolding of God's plan for your life. Your talents are not static; they evolve and develop as you respond to God's call and seek to serve Him.

Consider the example of King David in the Bible. Initially, he was known as a shepherd boy, a seemingly humble role. However, God saw potential within David far beyond tending sheep. Through faith, courage, and obedience, David rose to become a king, a mighty warrior, and a gifted poet and musician. His talents evolved as God's plan for his life unfolded. This demonstrates that God can use any talent, no matter how seemingly insignificant, to accomplish His grand purposes. The seemingly small gifts can be instrumental in building His kingdom.

Similarly, think about the Apostle Paul. Before his conversion, he was a persecutor of Christians, vehemently opposed to the teachings of Jesus. However, after his transformative encounter with Christ, Paul's life took an unexpected turn. His passion, once used for destruction, was redirected to spread the Gospel. He became a prolific writer, a powerful orator, and a tireless missionary, using his unique gifts to build the early church. His transformation showcases the power of God to repurpose our talents for His divine purposes.

It's imperative to understand that identifying your gifts is not about self-promotion or personal gain. Rather, it's about discerning how God intends for you to use those gifts to serve Him and others. Consider your community, your church, your family, and your workplace. Where do you see opportunities to use your talents to make a positive impact? How can you use your gifts to bless others, to encourage them, to uplift them, and to point them towards Christ? The gifts you possess are not meant to be hidden away or kept for yourself. They are meant to be shared with the world, to be used to build God's kingdom and to make a difference in the lives of others.

This act of service brings immense fulfillment and deepens your relationship with God. It is in giving that we truly receive; it is in serving that we find our purpose. This is a journey of self-discovery, therefore, it is not a selfish pursuit. It's an act of obedience to God's call, a response to His love and grace. By identifying and utilizing your gifts, you become a more effective instrument in His hands, a channel of His love and compassion to a world in desperate need.

As you delve deeper into this process of identifying your spiritual gifts, remember to remain humble. Your talents are gifts from

God, not achievements you earned. Cultivate a spirit of gratitude, acknowledging God's hand in your life. Celebrate your strengths, but also recognize your limitations. Seek mentorship from others who have gone before you, who can provide guidance and support.

Above all, trust in God's plan for your life, knowing that He has equipped you with everything you need to fulfill His purpose. The journey may have its challenges, but with faith and perseverance, you will undoubtedly discover and utilize the amazing gifts He has given you, bringing glory to His name and making a lasting impact on the world. The path may not always be clear, but with prayerful reflection and a willingness to serve, the way will unfold before you. This journey is not just about uncovering your potential; it's about actively participating in God's plan for your life, using your unique gifts to bring hope, healing, and transformation to a world that desperately needs it. Embrace the journey with faith and courage, and watch as your life becomes a testament to God's unwavering love and your incredible potential.

Overcoming Limiting Beliefs

Building upon the foundation of recognizing your inherent worth and identifying your God-given gifts, we now confront a crucial obstacle on the path to fulfilling your potential: limiting beliefs. These insidious thoughts, often operating beneath the surface of consciousness, can subtly yet powerfully sabotage your progress. They whisper doubts, fuel fears, and ultimately hinder your ability to embrace the amazing life God has planned for you. Understanding and overcoming these limiting beliefs is paramount to unlocking your full potential and living a life of purpose and joy.

These limiting beliefs are not necessarily conscious choices; they are often deeply ingrained patterns of thinking that have developed over time, perhaps influenced by past experiences, negative self-talk, or even societal pressures. They might manifest as self-doubt, the fear of failure, a feeling of inadequacy, or a belief that you are somehow unworthy of success or happiness. These negative thought patterns can manifest in various ways, often subtly undermining your confidence and hindering your ability to take risks and pursue your dreams. You might find yourself constantly second-guessing your decisions, avoiding challenges, or settling for less than you deserve.

For example, consider the individual who harbors a deep-seated belief that they are not creative. This belief might stem from past experiences where their creative efforts were criticized or dismissed. As a result, they might avoid any activity that requires creative thinking, limiting their potential for artistic expression, innovative problem-solving, or even simply finding joy in creative hobbies. This limiting belief, however, is not a reflection of their inherent capabilities; it's a distortion of reality, a false narrative that needs to be challenged and replaced with a more accurate and empowering belief.

Another common limiting belief is the fear of failure. This fear, often rooted in a deep-seated need for approval or a fear of rejection, can paralyze individuals, preventing them from taking risks and pursuing their goals. The fear of failure can lead to procrastination, avoidance of challenges, and ultimately, a life lived far below one's potential. The individual, afraid of not meeting expectations, might stay in a stagnant situation rather than risk pursuing something more fulfilling. The truth is, failure is not the opposite of success; it's a stepping stone towards it. Through our failures, we learn, we grow, and we become stronger and wiser.

The good news is that these limiting beliefs, however ingrained, are not immutable. They are not fixed parts of your identity. They are simply thoughts, and as such, they can be challenged, reframed, and ultimately replaced with positive, empowering beliefs. The process of overcoming these limiting beliefs involves a conscious and deliberate effort to identify them, challenge their validity, and replace them with beliefs that align with God's truth and your inherent worth. This requires introspection, prayer, and a willingness to embrace a growth mindset.

One powerful tool in this process is the practice of daily affirmations. Affirmations are positive statements that, when repeated regularly, can reprogram your subconscious mind and replace negative thought patterns with positive ones. These are not empty platitudes; they are declarations of faith, statements that you believe to be true, even if they don't feel true in the beginning. The power of affirmations lies in their ability to shift your perspective, to gradually reshape your self-image, and to foster a mindset of confidence and belief in your God-given potential.

For instance, if you struggle with self-doubt, you might repeat affirmations such as, "I am capable and competent," "I am worthy of success," or "God has equipped me with everything I need to achieve my goals." If you are battling the fear of failure, you might affirm, "I am brave and resilient," "I learn from my mistakes," or "God is with me, even in difficult times." The key is to choose affirmations that resonate with your specific challenges and speak directly to the limiting beliefs you are seeking to overcome. Repeat these affirmations several times a day, ideally both in the morning and before bed. Write them down, say them out loud, or even meditate on them, allowing the words to sink deep into your heart and mind.

Beyond affirmations, engaging in regular prayer is crucial. Prayer is not just about asking God for things; it's about connecting with Him, seeking His guidance, and surrendering your anxieties and fears to His loving care. Through prayer, you can receive the strength and wisdom you need to confront your limiting beliefs and replace them with God's truth. Ask God to reveal any negative thought patterns that are hindering your growth and to give you the courage and faith to overcome them. Prayer is a powerful tool for cultivating a mindset of hope, trust, and gratitude, all essential elements in overcoming limiting beliefs and unlocking your full potential.

Remember, this is a journey, not a destination. There will be times when negative thoughts resurface. This is perfectly normal; it's part of the process. When this happens, simply acknowledge the thoughts without judgment, gently redirect your focus back to your affirmations and prayers, and reaffirm your belief in God's plan for your life. Be patient with yourself, and celebrate your progress, no matter how small. Remember, God's grace is sufficient, and His power is made perfect in weakness.

Overcoming limiting beliefs requires not only inner work but also outward action. Take steps toward your goals, however small. Start with one manageable step; don't try to tackle everything at once. As you take action, you will build momentum and gain confidence, further reinforcing the positive beliefs you are cultivating. This is a virtuous cycle: positive beliefs fuel action, and action reinforces positive beliefs.

Let's look at some practical examples. Suppose someone believes they are not worthy of love. This might stem from past hurtful relationships or a negative self-image. They can counteract this belief by focusing on affirmations like, "I am worthy of love and acceptance," "I am loved unconditionally by God," and "I attract healthy, loving relationships." They can also proactively engage in self-care, participate in social activities, and seek out supportive relationships to build evidence that contradicts their limiting belief. Through these actions, they build a tangible experience that strengthens their affirmation and weakens the negative belief.

Similarly, someone struggling with the belief that they're incapable of achieving their professional goals can use affirmations like, "I am capable of achieving great things," "I have the skills and talent necessary to succeed," and "God guides my path to success." They can then start taking concrete steps, such as enrolling in professional development courses, networking with people in their industry, or seeking out mentorship. These actions provide evidence to support the affirmation and erode the negative belief that they are incapable.

Finally, remember that seeking support is not a sign of weakness but a testament to your wisdom and courage. Surrounding yourself with a community of faith, seeking guidance from mentors and spiritual leaders, and sharing your struggles with trusted friends or family members can provide invaluable support and encouragement throughout this process. The journey to overcoming limiting beliefs can be challenging, but you don't have to walk it alone.

The path to unveiling your God-given potential is paved with both internal and external actions. By identifying and challenging your limiting beliefs, embracing daily affirmations, strengthening your relationship with God through prayer, and taking consistent action towards your goals, you will gradually transform your mindset and unlock the remarkable potential that God has placed within you.

This is not merely a self-improvement project; it's a spiritual journey of transformation, leading you to a life of purpose, joy, and fulfillment, ultimately bringing glory to God and making a positive impact on the world around you. The journey might be long and winding, but with God's grace and your unwavering perseverance, you will undoubtedly arrive at your destined place, a place of abundant life and limitless potential. Remember, God's love for you is unconditional and His power is limitless. Trust in His plan, and watch as He unfolds your amazing destiny.

Embracing Gods Purpose

Having identified and begun to dismantle those internal barriers—the limiting beliefs that hold us back—we now arrive at a pivotal juncture: surrendering to God's purpose. This isn't a passive resignation, a mere giving up; rather, it's an active, conscious choice to align your will with God's will. It's a decision to trust implicitly in His plan, even when the path ahead seems unclear or challenging. This act of surrender is the key that unlocks the door to a life of profound purpose and fulfillment.

The surrender we're discussing is not about relinquishing your dreams or aspirations. Instead, it's about offering them to God, placing them in His capable hands, allowing Him to refine, redirect, or amplify them according to His divine blueprint for your life. Think of it as presenting a beautifully crafted piece of pottery to the Master Potter, trusting Him to perfect its form and purpose. He knows the clay, He knows the fire, and He knows the ultimate design far better than we ever could.

This surrender often requires a significant shift in perspective. We live in a culture that champions self-reliance and personal control. We're taught to meticulously plan every aspect of our lives, to forge our own paths, to be masters of our own destiny. While ambition and initiative are certainly valuable qualities, unchecked self-reliance can lead to a sense of isolation and ultimately, prevent us from experiencing the true fullness of God's plan for our lives.

True surrender begins with humility. It requires acknowledging our limitations, admitting our inability to fully comprehend God's grand design, and accepting that His ways are higher than our ways (Isaiah 55:9). It involves letting go of the illusion of control, recognizing that we are not the authors of our own stories but rather, characters in a much larger, more compelling narrative written by the Divine Author.

How do we practically implement this surrender? The answer lies in prayer. Prayer is not simply a request list presented to a celestial vending machine; it's a profound and intimate conversation with the Creator of the universe. Through prayer, we open our hearts and minds to God's guidance, seeking His wisdom and direction in every aspect of our lives. We invite Him to reveal His purpose for us, to illuminate the path ahead, and to empower us to walk it with courage and faith.

Prayer, however, shouldn't be a passive activity. It's a dynamic exchange, a two-way street. We need to listen as well as speak. We must cultivate a quiet stillness within, creating space to hear God's gentle whispers amidst the noise of daily life. This requires intentional time spent in His presence, a deliberate effort to disconnect from the distractions of the world and connect with the source of all wisdom and guidance. Journaling your prayers and reflections can be a powerful tool in this process, allowing you to track God's leading and witness His faithfulness over time.

It's crucial to understand that God's timing is perfect, even if it doesn't align with our expectations. Surrender often means waiting patiently, trusting that God is working behind the scenes, orchestrating events according to His perfect plan. This waiting period can be challenging, testing our faith and patience. However, it is during these times of seeming inactivity that God often works most profoundly, shaping our character, strengthening our faith, and preparing us for the tasks ahead.

Remember the parable of the sower and the seed (Matthew 13:1-23)? Some seeds fell on rocky ground, some among thorns, and some were eaten by birds. Only those seeds that fell on good soil produced a bountiful harvest. Similarly, our receptiveness to God's purpose depends on the condition of our hearts. Are we prepared to receive His plan? Are we willing to nurture the seed of His purpose, allowing it to take root and grow in the fertile ground of our surrendered hearts?

The path to embracing God's purpose is rarely straightforward. There will be obstacles, detours, and moments of doubt. But remember, God's grace is sufficient for every challenge. His strength is made perfect in our weakness (2 Corinthians 12:9). Lean on Him during those times of uncertainty; He will guide your steps, strengthen your resolve, and equip you with the necessary wisdom and resources to overcome any hurdle.

Consider aligning your goals with God's purpose. This is a crucial step in the process of surrender. Identify your passions, your talents, and your aspirations. Then, prayerfully consider how these gifts can be utilized to serve God and bless others. Are there ways you can use your skills to help the less fortunate, to spread the Gospel, or to make a positive impact on your community? Perhaps you're called to a specific ministry, a particular profession, or a unique avenue of service. The possibilities are limitless.

Surrender is not about becoming a passive observer in your own life; it's about becoming an active participant in God's grand design. It's about embracing your God-given potential and utilizing your talents and gifts to fulfill His purpose. This active participation requires faith, courage, and a willingness to step outside your comfort zone. It might involve taking risks, making sacrifices, and pursuing paths that seem unconventional or even daunting.

As you embark on this journey of surrender, remember that you are not alone. God is with you every step of the way. He is your guide, your strength, and your unwavering support. He walks alongside you, providing encouragement, guidance, and the grace you need to overcome any obstacles. Don't be afraid to ask for help from other believers. Surround yourself with a community of faith, seeking wise counsel and accountability as you navigate this transformative process.

This journey of surrender is a lifelong commitment, a continuous process of refining our hearts and aligning our wills with God's. It's a journey marked by both triumphs and challenges, moments of clarity and periods of doubt. But through it all, God's unwavering love remains our constant anchor, His grace our unfailing strength, and His purpose our ultimate destination.

The beauty of surrendering to God's plan is that it ultimately leads to a life of unparalleled joy, peace, and fulfillment. When we relinquish our need to control every aspect of our lives and trust in God's sovereign hand, we experience a freedom that surpasses all understanding. We find our true identity, our deepest purpose, and a sense of belonging that is both profound and enduring.

This surrender, this conscious relinquishing of self-will to God's perfect will, is the pathway to unlocking the boundless potential He has placed within you. It's a path paved with faith, trust, and unwavering perseverance. It's a path that may not always be easy, but it is undoubtedly a path worth walking, a path that leads to a life of immeasurable blessings and a legacy that will extend far beyond your earthly existence. Embrace this journey. Trust in God's perfect plan, and allow Him to unfold the magnificent destiny He has designed for you. It's a journey that will transform not only your life but also the lives of those around you. Remember, you are deeply loved, infinitely valued, and uniquely equipped for the purpose God has called you to fulfill. The adventure awaits.

Biblical Examples of Overcoming

The unwavering faith and perseverance demonstrated by biblical figures serve as powerful testaments to the transformative power of God. Their stories, etched in scripture, offer invaluable lessons and inspiration for navigating life's inevitable challenges. These individuals, faced with adversity of unimaginable proportions, demonstrate that even in the darkest of times, unwavering faith can lead to extraordinary triumphs. Their lives serve not only as examples of overcoming obstacles but also as blueprints for unlocking our own God-given potential. Let us delve into the lives of several key figures, exploring how their faith propelled them through hardship and ultimately led to remarkable achievements.

Joseph, a young man favored by his father but cruelly betrayed by his brothers, provides a compelling case study in faith amidst profound adversity. Sold into slavery, falsely accused, and unjustly imprisoned, Joseph's journey was far from easy. Yet, through it all, he maintained an unwavering faith in God's plan. He didn't succumb to bitterness or despair; instead, he chose to trust in God's sovereignty, even when the circumstances seemed utterly hopeless. His unwavering commitment to righteousness, even in the face of immense injustice, is a powerful reminder of the importance of maintaining moral integrity, even when it's difficult. Joseph's story highlights the transformative power of forgiveness, as he ultimately forgave his brothers for their heinous act of betrayal, demonstrating a level of compassion that is both remarkable and inspiring. His elevation from a slave to second-in-command in Egypt wasn't a result of luck or mere coincidence but a testament to his unwavering faith and God's faithfulness in fulfilling His promises.

His perseverance in the face of relentless hardship is a beacon of hope, demonstrating that even the deepest trials can be overcome through faith and trust in God's plan. Joseph's ability to find purpose and meaning, even in the midst of suffering, is a powerful lesson for us all. He didn't allow his circumstances to define him; he allowed his faith to shape his response, transforming adversity into an opportunity for God to work mightily in his life and the lives of others. His life serves as a profound reminder that God can and will use even our deepest sorrows to bring about His purposes.

The life of David, the shepherd boy who became king, offers another compelling illustration of overcoming adversity through faith and perseverance. Initially, David was overlooked, a seemingly insignificant figure compared to his older brothers. Yet, he possessed a deep faith in God and an unwavering confidence in His plan for his life. His courageous defeat of Goliath, a seemingly insurmountable giant, serves as a symbol of faith's ability to overcome seemingly impossible obstacles. This victory, achieved not through brute strength but through unwavering trust in God, established David as a figure of courage and faith. However, David's journey wasn't without its struggles. He faced betrayal, war, and internal conflicts that tested his faith repeatedly. Yet, throughout these turbulent periods, David consistently turned to God for guidance and strength. His psalms, expressions of his personal struggles and triumphs, offer a window into his deeply spiritual life. They reveal a man who experienced profound joy and devastating sorrow, yet consistently sought solace and strength in his relationship with God. David's life, far from being a flawless fairytale, is a realistic portrayal of a man wrestling with his imperfections while striving to live according to God's will. His story is a powerful reminder that God uses flawed people to accomplish great things. It's a powerful message of hope for anyone feeling inadequate or unworthy. God's grace is sufficient, even for those who struggle with their own failings, showing us that our imperfections do not disqualify us from His purpose. David's repentance, his heartfelt confessions of his mistakes, demonstrate a humility that is essential for spiritual growth. His life teaches us the importance of humility, accountability, and the transformative power of repentance.

Consider also the story of Esther, a young Jewish woman who courageously risked her life to save her people from annihilation. Facing a seemingly insurmountable challenge – the decree of Haman, the king's advisor, to exterminate the Jews – Esther, through her faith and courage, acted decisively. Her willingness to put herself in harm's way for the sake of her people demonstrates the power of faith to inspire extraordinary acts of courage. Her actions were not impulsive but born of a deep faith and trust in God's plan. Esther's story highlights the importance of courage in the face of adversity and the potential for seemingly insignificant individuals to make a profound difference in the world. It's a reminder that God can use anyone, regardless of their background or social standing, to bring about His purposes. Her story is a powerful testament to the potential that exists within each of us to impact the world around us. Her actions are a timeless example of courageous faith, proving that faith isn't passive acceptance but active engagement in the face of challenges. Esther's story reminds us that God often calls us to act courageously, even when the risks seem immense. It is a call to step outside our comfort zones and to trust in God's providence even when the outcome is uncertain.

These biblical narratives illustrate a common thread: unwavering faith in God's plan, even amidst overwhelming challenges. Joseph's perseverance in slavery, David's courage against Goliath and his battles against internal struggles, and Esther's courageous defiance—all demonstrate the power of faith to overcome seemingly insurmountable obstacles. These examples aren't merely historical accounts; they are living testimonies, vibrant illustrations of the power of faith to transform lives. They serve as a powerful inspiration for us today, reminding us that our potential is far greater than we often realize, and that with God's help, we too can overcome any obstacle that stands in our way. The challenges we face may be different from those faced by Joseph, David, or Esther, but the principles that guided them—faith, perseverance, and trust in God's plan—remain eternally relevant.

Moreover, these biblical figures demonstrate that overcoming adversity is not a solitary endeavor; it's a journey undertaken with

God as our constant companion. It requires faith, not as a passive belief, but as an active trust in God's unwavering love, power, and guidance. It demands perseverance, a steadfast commitment to the path God has laid out for us, even when faced with setbacks and disappointments. And it necessitates reliance on God's strength, acknowledging our own limitations and leaning on Him for the strength and wisdom to navigate the complexities of life. These individuals demonstrate that our struggles are not meant to defeat us; rather, they are opportunities for growth, refinement, and the ultimate unfolding of our God-given potential.

Their stories are not mere tales of the past; they are living examples, timeless narratives that resonate deeply with the human experience. They teach us that challenges are inevitable, but defeat is optional. Through faith and perseverance, even the most daunting obstacles can be overcome. The journey may be arduous, the path may be unclear, but with God as our guide, we can confidently navigate the complexities of life and unlock the boundless potential He has placed within us. The stories of Joseph, David, and Esther, among countless others, serve as beacons of hope, reminding us that with God, all things are possible. Embrace the challenges, trust in God's plan, and let your faith be the compass guiding you towards the fulfillment of your God-given potential. The journey will be transformative, not only for you but for those whose lives you will touch along the way. Your unique purpose, waiting to be unveiled, is a testament to God's incredible love and plan for your life. Dare to believe in your potential, for it is a divine gift, a masterpiece waiting to be revealed.

Taking Calculated Risks

Stepping out in faith often requires us to embrace calculated risks. This isn't about reckless abandon, but about discerning opportunities that align with God's purpose for our lives and taking measured steps toward them, even when fear whispers doubts in our ears. It's about recognizing that growth rarely occurs within the confines of our comfort zones. Think of a seed; it must break free from the protective shell to sprout, grow, and ultimately bear fruit.

Similarly, we must be willing to break free from the familiar to embrace the potential that lies beyond. This process begins with prayerful discernment. Before taking any significant step, spend time in quiet contemplation, seeking God's guidance. Ask for wisdom, clarity, and the courage to act. Read scripture, meditate on relevant passages, and listen for the gentle promptings of the Holy Spirit. This isn't about forcing a decision; it's about patiently waiting for God's confirmation. Consider journaling your thoughts and prayers. Writing down your feelings, fears, and aspirations can help you process them and gain perspective.

Identifying manageable risks involves careful assessment. We're not called to be foolhardy, but to be wise and discerning. This requires honestly evaluating our strengths and weaknesses. What resources do we have at our disposal? What support systems can we rely on? What are the potential pitfalls, and how might we mitigate them?

It's helpful to create a pros and cons list, weighing the potential benefits against the possible challenges. Remember, even seemingly small steps can have significant consequences, so thorough consideration is crucial.

Consider the example of a young entrepreneur with a brilliant business idea. Fear may whisper doubts about his skills, resources, and market viability. However, a calculated risk might involve launching a small-scale pilot program, testing the market, gathering feedback, and securing a small amount of funding to prove the concept before committing fully. This is a far cry from reckless risk-taking. It's a measured approach, taking a tentative step while remaining prepared for various outcomes. Through this process, he demonstrates his initiative and proactive faith in God's guidance.

Another crucial element is developing a robust action plan. Once a decision has been made, it's vital to outline the steps needed to achieve the goal. This plan should be detailed, realistic, and time-bound. Break down large, overwhelming tasks into smaller, manageable steps. This makes the process less daunting and provides a sense of accomplishment as each step is completed. This structured approach demonstrates a commitment to the goal and a proactive faith that allows God's blessings to flow.

Consider a couple considering a mission trip to a remote village. Their action plan could include fundraising, securing visas, researching health precautions, contacting local missionaries, and planning their itinerary. Each step, meticulously planned, demonstrates their commitment and deepens their faith in God's provision. The very act of planning demonstrates a faith that God will provide the necessary resources and opportunities to successfully complete their mission.

Remember, the action plan should be flexible. Unexpected challenges will inevitably arise. Therefore, building in contingencies and remaining adaptable is vital. Remain open to adjustments and redirection as God reveals His path. Sometimes, the most challenging aspects of the journey can lead to unexpected blessings and opportunities that could never have been foreseen through meticulous planning.

Furthermore, seeking counsel from trusted mentors or spiritual advisors is essential. Sharing your plans and concerns with someone who can offer wisdom and support can provide valuable insights and encouragement. Their perspective can help you identify potential blind spots and refine your approach. Surrounding yourself with people who support your vision and will pray for you is crucial to building perseverance, especially during challenging times. Their prayers and words of encouragement are powerful tools in reinforcing faith during difficult moments.

Building a strong support network is a proactive demonstration of faith. It acknowledges that we are not meant to journey alone, but that God provides people to walk alongside us, offering encouragement, advice and prayers. These individuals can serve as accountability partners, offering encouragement when doubt creeps in, and helping us stay focused on our objectives. Their support isn't merely emotional, it's also practical, as they may offer assistance with resources, skills or even financial support.

Remember that setbacks are inevitable. Even the most carefully planned ventures may encounter obstacles. When these happen, it's crucial not to lose heart. Instead, view these challenges as opportunities for growth and learning. Reflect on what went wrong, make necessary adjustments, and continue moving forward with renewed determination and faith. This is where true faith is tested and refined, building strength and resilience for future endeavours.

The process of taking calculated risks is not merely about achieving goals; it's about deepening our faith and trust in God. It's about surrendering our fears to His love and allowing Him to guide our steps. It's about recognizing that His provision is not limited to material blessings but also encompasses wisdom, guidance, and the strength to persevere. Every step taken in faith, regardless of the outcome, is a testament to our trust in Him and an act of worship.

As we step out in faith, we are not simply pursuing personal ambitions; we are fulfilling God's purpose for our lives. We are contributing to His kingdom and making a difference in the world.

This perspective transforms seemingly ordinary challenges into opportunities to showcase God's love and grace. Remember that the greatest risks often lead to the greatest rewards, and the most profound growth comes from stepping outside of our comfort zones and trusting in God's unwavering love and guidance. Embrace the journey, celebrate the victories, and learn from the setbacks, always remembering that God is with you, every step of the way. He will never leave you nor forsake you.

The journey of faith is a lifelong pursuit, a continuous process of learning, growing, and trusting in God's plan. Taking calculated risks is not a one-time event but a recurring theme that will appear throughout our lives. Each challenge presents an opportunity to deepen our faith and develop our reliance on God's unwavering support. Therefore, approach each risk with prayerful consideration, careful planning, and unwavering trust in God's guidance. His provision is limitless, and His grace is sufficient for every challenge we face. He is our strength, our comfort, and our guide. Embrace the journey, for it is a journey of faith, growth, and abundant blessings. God's blessings are abundant and plentiful for those who trust in Him.

Remember the parable of the talents in Matthew 25. The master entrusted his servants with varying amounts of talents, and those who invested their talents wisely were rewarded. This reflects the importance of taking calculated risks, investing our time, abilities, and resources in opportunities that align with God's purpose. It is not about fearing failure, but about embracing the possibility of success, knowing that our efforts are guided by a loving and all-powerful God. Therefore, let us not be held back by fear, but motivated by faith, daring to venture into uncharted territory, trusting in the divine guidance that leads us towards a life of purpose and fulfillment.

Finally, remember that even when things don't go as planned, even when setbacks occur, our faith remains a constant. God is faithful, even when we are not. He is a God of second chances, of restoration, and of new beginnings. Therefore, do not let fear paralyze you. Do not let setbacks discourage you. Instead, trust in God's unwavering love and faithfulness, and continue to take those calculated risks, knowing that even in failure, there is growth and a deeper understanding of God's plan for your life. The journey is just as important as the destination. The process of growth, trust, and faith in God is a lifelong journey, and each step, however small, brings you closer to the fulfillment of God's purpose in your life. Embrace the journey, and trust in God's perfect timing and perfect plan.

Seeking Mentorship and Support

Stepping out in faith is rarely a solitary endeavor. While the ultimate reliance is on God, the journey is often enriched and sustained by the presence of others who understand, encourage, and support your efforts. Building a strong support network is not merely beneficial; it is essential for navigating the challenges and celebrating the triumphs inherent in pursuing God's calling. This network serves as a vital anchor, providing stability and strength during times of uncertainty and doubt.

The first step in building this vital network is actively seeking mentorship. Mentorship is not about finding someone to do the work for you, but finding someone who has walked a similar path, someone who can offer wisdom gleaned from experience, someone who can provide guidance and perspective you might not yet possess. This mentor doesn't need to be a renowned figure; it could be a trusted elder in your church, a respected colleague, or even a friend who has demonstrated strength and resilience in their own faith journey. The key is to find someone whose life reflects the values and character you aspire to embody.

Consider what qualities you seek in a mentor. Look for someone who demonstrates spiritual maturity, integrity, and a genuine commitment to their faith. Look for someone who is willing to invest their time and energy in guiding you. Look for someone who will challenge you to grow, yet who will also offer compassion and understanding during times of struggle. Don't be afraid to approach potential mentors; express your admiration for their faith and your desire for their guidance. Be prepared to be vulnerable and honest about your aspirations and challenges. Remember, the most effective mentoring relationships are built on mutual respect and trust. A good mentor will reciprocate your openness and willingness to learn.

Beyond mentorship, actively cultivate relationships with like-minded individuals who share your faith and your aspirations. This could involve joining a small group within your church, participating in Bible studies, or connecting with others who are pursuing similar goals. These relationships provide a vital source of encouragement, accountability, and fellowship. Surrounding yourself with people who share your values reinforces your commitment to your faith journey and provides a space for mutual support and shared experiences. Sharing your struggles and victories with others who understand will significantly lighten your load and prevent feelings of isolation.

Consider the power of shared prayer. Engaging in prayer with others—whether it's within a small group or with a close friend—creates a powerful bond and strengthens your faith. Shared prayer offers comfort, guidance, and the reassurance that you are not alone in your struggles. It fosters a sense of community and mutual support, reinforcing your connection with God and with other believers.

Building a strong support system also necessitates being accountable. This means sharing your goals and progress with your mentor and your community of faith. This accountability keeps you focused, prevents procrastination, and provides a system of checks and balances, ensuring you stay on track with your spiritual goals.

Honest accountability keeps us grounded and prevents us from becoming complacent or straying from our path. A trustworthy confidant can gently correct us, point out areas where we falter, and provide the necessary support to help us get back on track when we stumble.

However, remember that building a support network is a two-way street. It's not just about receiving support; it's also about giving it. As you grow in your faith, you will naturally find yourself in a position to offer encouragement, guidance, and support to others. This reciprocal nature strengthens the bonds within your network and creates a vibrant, supportive community where everyone feels valued and empowered. Sharing your experiences and offering encouragement to others deepens your own understanding and strengthens your own faith. Helping others strengthens the bonds within the community and further solidifies your commitment to the larger body of believers.

Remember that vulnerability is key. Sharing your struggles and doubts with trusted individuals is not a sign of weakness; it is a sign of strength. Openness and honesty create deeper connections and foster a more authentic community. When you share your challenges, you invite others to share theirs, creating a space of empathy and mutual understanding. It helps build a closer relationship with your mentor and members of your community who care about your faith journey. This shared vulnerability strengthens the bonds and builds trust among all participants.

Choosing your support system wisely is also important. Ensure that those you surround yourself with are truly supportive and encouraging, not those who would derail your spiritual journey. This means actively discerning between individuals who truly uplift you in your pursuit of faith, and those who may discourage or distract you from your path. While we should be compassionate and understanding of the struggles others face, we must also prioritize those relationships that promote our spiritual well-being. We need to be mindful of those that may create unnecessary conflict or hinder our relationship with God.

Beyond individual mentors and small groups, consider broader communities that align with your faith and values. These could include organizations dedicated to social justice, missions work, or charitable endeavors. Participating in these activities expands your circle of support, providing additional opportunities for growth and connection. Contributing to a cause larger than yourself can be immensely rewarding, providing a renewed sense of purpose and enriching your faith journey. It provides a platform to put your faith into action, and a wider context to understand how your faith interacts with the real world and the challenges it poses. Remember, building this support network is an ongoing process.

Relationships should flow, and you may find yourself needing to adjust or expand your network over time. Be open to new connections and be willing to let go of relationships that no longer serve your spiritual growth. Cultivating meaningful connections is a lifelong journey, and your support network should evolve alongside your journey of faith. Continuously nurturing these relationships is vital in ensuring that you maintain a strong support system that can help you navigate the challenges and celebrate the victories along the way. Be patient and persistent in this process, and trust that God will guide you towards the relationships that will best serve you on your path.

Finally, remember that the ultimate source of support and strength is God Himself. Your relationship with God should always be the cornerstone of your faith journey. The support network you build serves to enhance and strengthen that relationship, providing encouragement and guidance along the way, but it should never replace the central role of your relationship with God. As you seek mentorship and support, continuously seek God's guidance. Pray for wisdom in selecting mentors and building your network, and trust that He will lead you to the people and communities that will best support your journey. The power of prayer, and daily seeking guidance from God, will greatly enhance your ability to build a support system that strengthens your path to your spiritual goals.

Your journey of faith is a lifelong process, and cultivating these supportive relationships will provide strength, encouragement, and stability along this path.

Handling Criticism and Rejection

Stepping out in faith often means facing criticism and rejection. This isn't a sign that you're doing something wrong; rather, it's a common experience for anyone who dares to pursue God's calling with boldness. The path to fulfilling your purpose is rarely smooth; expect bumps, detours, and perhaps even some harsh headwinds. Learning to navigate these challenges with grace and resilience is crucial to persevering and ultimately achieving your goals, whatever those might be in God's design for you.

The first step in handling criticism is to recognize its source. Sometimes, criticism is well-intentioned, though poorly delivered. A friend or family member might voice concern, stemming from a place of love, but their words might come across as harsh or judgmental. Learning to discern the intent behind the criticism is vital. Try to understand their perspective and the reasons for their concerns. This doesn't mean you have to agree with everything they say, but understanding the source of their words can help you respond with empathy and grace. Remember, even the most well-meaning critique can feel hurtful, so patience and understanding are crucial.

On the other hand, criticism can be rooted in malice or envy. Not everyone will be supportive of your faith journey. Some may even actively try to discourage you. It's important to develop a thick skin and not let these negative voices consume you. Remember that their opinions are not a reflection of your worth or your God-given potential. Proverbs 17:22 reminds us, "A cheerful heart is good medicine, but a crushed spirit dries up the bones." Protecting your heart and maintaining a positive mindset is paramount to navigating negativity.

When faced with criticism, take time to assess its validity. Is there any truth to the criticism? Can you learn from it and grow? Even negative feedback can sometimes contain valuable insights. Seek out constructive criticism. This might involve asking trusted mentors or friends for their honest opinions and feedback. Be open to hearing what they have to say, even if it is difficult to hear. Use their insights as an opportunity for personal growth and development, ensuring that you are being led by God in your endeavor.

Rejection, too, is an inevitable part of the journey. You might face rejection from potential partners, employers, or even within your faith community. This rejection can feel deeply personal, threatening your sense of self-worth and purpose. Remember that rejection is not a reflection of your inherent value. God's love is unconditional; it doesn't depend on your achievements or the approval of others. His acceptance is your ultimate anchor.

In the face of rejection, it's important to lean on your faith and trust in God's plan. Jeremiah 29:11 assures us, "For I know the plans I have for you," declares the Lord, "plans to prosper you and not to harm you, plans to give you hope and a future." This promise is not a guarantee of easy success; it's a promise of God's unwavering love and support, even amidst setbacks.

Cultivate a mindset of resilience. View setbacks as opportunities for learning and growth. Instead of dwelling on what went wrong, focus on what you can learn from the experience. What could you have done differently? How can you grow stronger and wiser from this challenge? What positive aspects can you take forward?

Seeking professional help can be invaluable during these times. A counselor or therapist can provide a safe space to process your emotions and develop healthy coping mechanisms. They can help you navigate the complexities of dealing with criticism and rejection, helping you to maintain emotional balance and positive self-esteem. Remember that seeking help is a sign of strength, not weakness. The people of God often support one another.

Building a strong support network is critical in navigating these difficult emotions. Surround yourself with people who uplift and encourage you, who see your worth and potential regardless of external validation. Share your struggles with these trusted individuals; allow them to offer comfort, support and encouragement. Remember, sharing your burdens lightens the load. True friends will be there for you regardless of the outcome of your efforts.

Maintaining a positive mindset is crucial. Practice gratitude; focus on the blessings in your life, however small they may seem. Spend time in prayer and meditation; allow yourself to reconnect with God's presence and His peace. Remember that God sees your heart and your intentions. His love is unconditional and unwavering, regardless of the opinions of others. Lean on scripture, drawing strength and comfort from His word. Focus on the positive actions that you have taken, and how your faith has led you to this point.

Learning to handle criticism and rejection is a lifelong process. It requires patience, perseverance, and a deep reliance on God's grace. Don't allow these challenges to define you; instead, let them refine you, strengthen your faith, and propel you forward on your journey of purpose. Remember that you are not alone; God is with you every step of the way. His strength will empower you to handle any obstacle that you encounter. It is in these challenges that your faith will be tested and grow stronger. His plan for you is ultimately one of hope, even when faced with difficult times. Remember your purpose, remain focused, and trust in the journey. God's timing is perfect, even if it doesn't feel that way in the midst of trials.

It is also important to understand that sometimes, criticism and rejection are opportunities for redirection. God may be leading you in a different direction, and the obstacles you face are His way of guiding you towards a path that aligns more closely with His purpose for your life. Be open to change and trust that God's plans are always greater than your own. This may involve altering your plans or changing your approach. Reflect on whether your current direction is still aligned with your values and with the guidance of the Holy Spirit. Be willing to adjust your course as needed.

One of the most powerful weapons against negativity is forgiveness. Forgive those who criticize or reject you. Holding onto resentment and bitterness will only hurt you in the long run. Forgiveness is not about condoning their actions; it's about releasing the anger and bitterness that consume you. Forgiveness allows you to move forward, free from the weight of negativity. It is a freeing act that will help to cleanse your heart.

Finally, remember to celebrate your victories, no matter how small. Acknowledge the progress you've made and give thanks to God for His guidance and support. Celebrating small wins will keep you motivated and energized as you continue your journey. Recognizing milestones, big and small, will reinforce your faith and confidence. These accomplishments are not just your own; they are evidence of God's working in your life. Sharing these triumphs with your support network will help you to stay positive and centered. Giving thanks and celebrating success are crucial to maintaining a positive outlook, especially when the path isn't always easy. Remember that God's hand is guiding you, and that you are on the right path. Trust in the journey and celebrate the wins along the way, even if they seem small in the grand scheme of things.

Celebrating Small Victories

We often focus on the grand, sweeping victories in life, the monumental achievements that seem to mark our progress with bold exclamation points. But what about the quiet, subtle wins? The small, seemingly insignificant moments of progress that, when accumulated, form the bedrock of our larger successes? These are the victories we must learn to celebrate with equal, if not greater, fervor. It is in these small triumphs that we truly see God's hand at work, gently guiding us along our path.

Think about it: the day you finally overcame a persistent negative thought pattern, replacing it with a positive affirmation and a grateful heart. Or the moment you resisted the temptation to indulge in an unhealthy habit, choosing instead to prioritize your well-being. Perhaps it was the completion of a small task that had been looming over you, a weight lifted from your shoulders. These are not merely minor incidents; they are significant steps toward a greater purpose. They are evidence of your growth, your resilience, and God's unwavering grace.

Failing to acknowledge these small victories is like trying to climb a mountain without pausing to appreciate the stunning views from each conquered vantage point. We become so focused on the summit that we miss the beauty of the journey, the strength we've gained with each step, the lessons we've learned along the way. Celebrating the small wins is crucial for maintaining momentum and keeping our spirits high, especially during challenging times.

One highly effective method for celebrating these small achievements is to keep a gratitude journal. This isn't about listing only the "big" things—the new house, the promotion, the exciting trip. Instead, it's about capturing the everyday blessings, the quiet moments of joy and peace that often go unnoticed. Did you have a particularly meaningful conversation with a loved one? Did you feel an unexpected surge of inspiration or creativity? Did you manage to complete a challenging project despite feeling overwhelmed?

Record these moments in your journal. Write about them in detail, recalling the feelings and sensations you experienced. By regularly documenting these small victories, you create a powerful record of God's faithfulness in your life. You begin to notice patterns of blessing, evidence of God's unwavering presence and guidance. This consistent practice cultivates a spirit of thankfulness, transforming your perspective from one of scarcity and struggle to one of abundance and gratitude. Over time, this practice will shift your focus from what's lacking to what you already possess – the immeasurable gifts of God's love and grace.

This isn't merely about positive thinking; it's about recognizing God's active participation in your life, however subtle it may seem. When you celebrate your small wins, you're not just acknowledging your own accomplishments; you're recognizing the divine hand that guided and empowered you. You're expressing gratitude for the unseen forces that worked behind the scenes, orchestrating the events that led to your success.

Consider this: a single drop of water may seem insignificant, but countless drops together form a mighty river. Similarly, seemingly insignificant achievements, when celebrated and accumulated, create a powerful current of momentum propelling you towards your goals. Each small victory strengthens your faith, boosts your confidence, and instills a sense of purpose. It fuels your determination to keep going, even when the road ahead seems daunting.

Another effective way to celebrate these small wins is to share them with others. Talk to a trusted friend, family member, or mentor. Describe the challenges you faced and the ways in which God helped you overcome them. Sharing your experiences not only reinforces your own sense of accomplishment, but it also inspires others to persevere in their own journeys. It fosters a sense of community and shared purpose, reminding us that we are not alone in our struggles and triumphs.

Let's illustrate this with some practical examples. Imagine you're working on a challenging project at work, a project that feels overwhelming and nearly impossible to complete. You break it down into smaller, more manageable tasks. Each time you finish a task, no matter how small, take a moment to acknowledge your accomplishment. Perhaps you light a candle, listen to your favorite uplifting music, or simply take a few deep breaths to appreciate your progress.

Another example: you've been struggling with a particular sin or bad habit. You experience a day or even just a few hours where you resist the temptation. That's a victory! Celebrate that victory. Thank God for His grace and strength. Journal about it. Share it with a trusted friend or mentor. Don't minimize the significance of that victory, for it's a step towards lasting transformation.

Think about the times you've shown kindness to someone in need, even a small act of service. Perhaps you helped an elderly person cross the street, or you volunteered your time at a local charity.

These small acts of compassion, fueled by love and faith, are not only blessings to the recipients but also significant victories for you. They strengthen your character and deepen your connection to God and your community.

The key is to cultivate an attitude of gratitude, to actively seek out the good in each day, and to celebrate the small victories that often go unnoticed. This involves intentional mindfulness, taking time to reflect on your day and acknowledging the progress you've made, no matter how incremental. It's about shifting your focus from what's lacking to what you already possess – the abundant grace and blessings God has bestowed upon you.

Celebrating these small victories is not about self-congratulation or arrogance. It's about fostering a thankful heart, recognizing God's hand in your life, and maintaining the momentum needed to persevere on your faith journey. It's about cultivating an attitude of hope and gratitude, even amidst challenges and setbacks. It's about recognizing the power of small steps, and the significance of consistent effort, guided by faith and fueled by God's love.

Remember that faith is a journey, not a destination. There will be times of doubt, discouragement, and even failure. But by acknowledging and celebrating the small victories along the way, you build resilience, strengthen your faith, and maintain the energy needed to continue pressing forward. Trust in God's plan for your life, and remember that even the smallest step taken in faith is a significant victory worth celebrating. These small victories are not just stepping stones; they are beacons of hope, shining brightly on the path to your ultimate destination. Embrace them, cherish them, and allow them to fuel your continued journey of faith.

Biblical Examples of Faith in Action

The lives of biblical figures offer a rich tapestry of faith in action, showcasing the diverse ways in which individuals responded to God's call and overcame adversity. Their stories aren't simply historical accounts; they are living, breathing examples of how unwavering faith, even amidst the most challenging circumstances, can lead to remarkable results. These individuals didn't always experience immediate, dramatic answers to their prayers; rather, their faith was often tested, refined, and strengthened through prolonged periods of trial and tribulation. It is in these trials that their faith truly shines, revealing the depth of their commitment and the power of their trust in God's plan.

Consider Abraham, the father of faith. God's call to leave his homeland, his family, and all that he knew was a profound act of faith. He didn't know where he was going, nor what awaited him in the promised land. Yet, he obeyed without hesitation, demonstrating an unwavering trust in God's promises, even when those promises seemed improbable. His journey was marked by periods of doubt and uncertainty, but his faith persevered, ultimately culminating in the birth of Isaac, a testament to God's faithfulness. Abraham's faith wasn't passive; it was active, demanding obedience, sacrifice, and a willingness to relinquish control to a higher power. He learned to trust in God's timing and providence, even when the path forward seemed shrouded in mystery. His willingness to offer his son, Isaac, as a sacrifice, stands as a powerful example of absolute faith and obedience, a stark demonstration of his commitment to God's will above all else. This act, though seemingly brutal, reveals the depths of his faith and his unwavering belief in God's ultimate plan.

Joseph, another prominent figure in the Old Testament, provides another compelling example of faith in action. Sold into slavery by his own brothers, enduring years of unjust imprisonment, and facing seemingly insurmountable obstacles, Joseph never lost sight of God's presence in his life. His unwavering faith, his steadfast refusal to compromise his integrity, and his persistent trust in God's ultimate plan allowed him to not only survive but to thrive. His eventual elevation to second in command in Egypt, a position of power and influence, wasn't merely a stroke of good fortune; it was a direct result of his faithfulness to God. Joseph's ability to forgive his brothers, who had wronged him so deeply, demonstrates a profound level of grace and compassion, reflecting the transformative power of faith. His actions serve as a testament to the power of forgiveness and the capacity for human transformation through faith in God. He didn't wallow in self-pity or bitterness; instead, he chose to see God's hand at work, even in the midst of his suffering. His story serves as an inspiring example of how faith can transform adversity into opportunity.

The life of Moses, the prophet who led the Israelites out of slavery in Egypt, is a remarkable illustration of faith conquering seemingly insurmountable obstacles. Facing the formidable power of Pharaoh and the might of the Egyptian army, Moses, armed with nothing but his faith in God, stood firm in his conviction. His unwavering belief in God's power, his courage to challenge the status quo, and his perseverance in the face of adversity, ultimately led to the liberation of his people. The parting of the Red Sea, a miraculous event described in Exodus, is a testament to the power of faith and God's intervention in human affairs. Moses's leadership, guided by his deep faith in God's plan, demonstrated the transformative power of faith in shaping history. It highlights the fact that even when facing overwhelming odds, unwavering faith can lead to extraordinary results. The story isn't just about escaping slavery, but about trusting God's promise of a better future, even when the present circumstances are overwhelmingly bleak.

David, the shepherd boy who became king, provides another compelling example of faith in action. His courageous confrontation with Goliath, a seemingly invincible giant, exemplifies the power of faith to overcome fear and doubt. David, armed with nothing but his sling and his unwavering faith in God, faced the formidable warrior, relying not on his own strength but on God's strength. His victory wasn't simply a physical triumph; it was a spiritual victory, a testament to the power of faith to overcome even the most daunting challenges. David's life, however, was not without its trials and tribulations. He faced betrayal, adversity, and conflict, but his faith in God remained steadfast. Even his repentance when he made mistakes demonstrates his reliance on God's grace. Through his journey, David showed that faith isn't about being perfect, but about continually striving to live according to God's will and seeking forgiveness when we fall short. His example is a powerful reminder that faith is not a shield against suffering, but a source of strength to endure it.

These are just a few examples of how biblical figures demonstrated faith in action. Their lives, filled with challenges, triumphs, and unwavering trust in God, provide a powerful blueprint for navigating our own lives with faith. Their stories aren't just historical narratives; they are practical guides, illustrating how faith can empower us to overcome adversity, achieve our goals, and ultimately, live a life pleasing to God. Each story reveals a different facet of faith, emphasizing the importance of obedience, perseverance, forgiveness, courage, and trust in God's timing and plan. By studying their lives and emulating their faith, we can cultivate our own faith, strengthening our ability to overcome challenges and live a life that is both meaningful and fulfilling. The common thread that binds these narratives together is the unwavering belief in a higher power, a trust that transcends human understanding and a reliance on God's grace to guide their steps. This unwavering faith, tested and refined through trials, ultimately emerges victorious, shaping not only their individual lives but also the course of history.

Their examples are not meant to suggest that life will be easy or without struggle. Quite the contrary, the lives of these figures demonstrate that faith is often tested and refined in the crucible of adversity. The point is not to avoid hardship but to approach it with unwavering faith, knowing that God's grace is sufficient and that even in the darkest moments, His light shines brightly. These individuals were not exempt from human failings; they made mistakes, faced temptation, and experienced setbacks. However, their response to these challenges, their ability to rise above adversity through faith, is what makes their stories so inspiring and so relevant to our own lives today.

The path of faith is rarely straightforward. There will be moments of doubt, times when the answers seem elusive, and periods when the path ahead appears shrouded in darkness. Yet, it is in these moments of uncertainty that our faith is tested and refined. By looking to the examples of these biblical figures, we gain the courage and strength to persevere, to trust in God's plan, and to remain steadfast in our faith, even when the road ahead seems daunting. Their stories are a constant reminder that faith is not a passive acceptance of fate, but an active engagement with God, a relentless pursuit of His will, and an unwavering trust in His promises. It's about surrendering to God's plan, even when that plan seems unclear or challenging. It is about maintaining faith and perseverance, even when faced with seemingly insurmountable obstacles.

The overarching lesson from these biblical examples of faith in action is that faith is not a static belief but a dynamic relationship with God. It's a journey of trust, obedience, and perseverance, marked by both triumphs and trials. It's about acknowledging God's sovereignty in our lives and surrendering our own will to His. It's about accepting His grace and forgiveness, even when we fall short.

It's about embracing the challenges and uncertainties of life, knowing that God is with us every step of the way. The lives of these individuals, though separated by time and circumstance, provide a timeless message: that unwavering faith, even in the face of overwhelming adversity, can lead to extraordinary results. Their stories remind us that our own journeys of faith, though unique, are not without precedent; they are connected to a rich history of faith, courage, and perseverance, offering guidance and inspiration as we navigate our own paths. Embrace the lessons learned from these biblical examples, and allow them to strengthen your faith, guide your steps, and empower you to live a life that is both meaningful and pleasing to God. The journey of faith is not a solitary one; it is a shared experience, strengthened by the examples and inspiration of those who have walked this path before us.

Defining Your Niche

Building a successful platform, whether it's a ministry, a coaching practice, or an online presence, requires a strategic approach. Just as a skilled craftsman carefully selects the finest materials for a masterpiece, so too must you carefully choose your niche – the specific area of expertise where you will focus your efforts. This isn't about limiting yourself; it's about sharpening your focus and maximizing your impact. Think of it as becoming a specialist, rather than a generalist, in the vast landscape of faith-based guidance and inspiration. The biblical accounts themselves showcase this principle; consider the diverse roles and callings of the apostles –each uniquely gifted and contributing their specific strengths to the early church. Each possessed a unique perspective and skillset which complemented the whole body of Christ. You too possess unique gifts and talents, honed by experience and guided by your faith, that are waiting to be discovered and deployed.

Identifying your niche involves a process of introspection and research. Begin by honestly assessing your strengths, passions, and experiences. What do you excel at? What brings you joy and fulfillment? What unique perspectives can you offer based on your life journey and relationship with God? Perhaps you have a knack for helping others overcome anxiety through prayer and meditation; maybe your expertise lies in fostering stronger marital relationships using biblical principles; or maybe you're gifted in guiding young adults through the challenges of navigating faith in a secular world.

Whatever your area of strength, it forms the foundation of your niche. Your unique perspective, shaped by your personal experiences with God and His guidance, becomes a powerful tool in ministering to those who share your struggles or long for the same blessings.

Don't underestimate the impact of your individual life journey as a testament to God's grace and power. It's in these authentic experiences where others see a reflection of their own stories and find hope.

Once you've identified your potential strengths, delve into thorough market research. This isn't simply about looking at competitor websites; it's about deeply understanding your target audience. Who are you trying to reach? What are their needs, desires, and pain points? What are their preferred methods of receiving information and support – online courses, workshops, books, one-on-one coaching, podcasts? Consider using online surveys, social media polls, or even informal conversations to gather data. The information you gather will help you tailor your messaging and your platform's content to resonate with their specific needs.

Understanding your audience allows you to connect with them on a deeper level, strengthening your rapport and building trust. This research is an act of faith—trusting that God has led you here for a specific reason and equipping you to fulfill His purpose. The market research phase also involves examining the competitive landscape. Who else is offering similar services or content in your chosen niche? What are their strengths and weaknesses? How can you differentiate yourself and offer something unique and valuable? This isn't about discouraging competition, but about strategically positioning yourself to attract your target audience effectively.

Instead of viewing competitors as adversaries, approach them as fellow ministers, each contributing to a larger tapestry of faith-based guidance. Their success doesn't detract from your potential; rather, it validates the need for your particular contribution. Observe what they do, where they excel, and most importantly, where there's room for improvement or a different approach. Finding your niche requires discernment, seeking God's guidance in determining the most effective way you can contribute to His Kingdom.

For example, let's say you're passionate about helping women navigate the challenges of motherhood while maintaining a strong spiritual life. Your market research might reveal a significant number of online resources for moms dealing with stress and time management, but a gap in resources focusing specifically on integrating faith-based practices into their daily routines. This gap presents a valuable opportunity to carve out your niche and offer a unique approach, one that blends practical advice with spiritual encouragement. It's about finding your unique contribution within a specific area of the broader faith-based landscape. Your passion and experience will fuel your creativity, providing insight and inspiration others seek. This isn't about inventing something entirely new; it's about creating something valuable and unique with your own distinct voice.

Another example might involve a passion for using biblical principles to improve personal finances. While many resources exist on personal finance, a niche could be developed focusing on stewardship from a faith-based perspective, emphasizing giving and tithing, ethical investing, and long-term financial planning aligned with biblical values. This focused approach differentiates you from secular financial advisors and appeals to a specific audience seeking a faith-integrated approach to personal wealth management. You are not simply offering financial advice; you are offering a holistic approach to wealth management grounded in biblical teachings. This niche allows you to connect with those seeking a faith-based lens to understand the financial aspect of life, understanding the stewardship God has placed in their care.

Defining your niche is an ongoing process, not a one-time event. As you gain experience and your audience grows, you may find opportunities to refine your focus or expand into related areas. However, starting with a well-defined niche provides a strong foundation for building a sustainable and impactful platform. Remember that your niche isn't a cage, but a launchpad. It provides a focused platform from which to share your gifts and talents and make a tangible difference in the lives of others. It allows you to speak directly to the needs of a specific audience, creating a stronger connection and better serving God's purpose. This commitment to a focused niche will increase your influence and broaden your sphere of reach. Your defined area of expertise becomes your unique contribution to the collective body of Christ.

As you continue to seek God's guidance and tailor your efforts to the specific needs of your audience, you will find an increasing sense of fulfillment and purpose in your ministry or platform. This process of defining your niche is a journey of discernment, a process of seeking God's guidance to discover the unique talents and experiences He has entrusted to you. It's about aligning your passions and skills with the needs of others, creating a synergistic relationship that benefits both you and those you serve. It's an act of faith, trusting that God has equipped you for a specific purpose, and that by focusing your energy and resources, you can achieve greater impact and fulfill that calling. The journey of faith is often one of refining our focus, learning to identify our unique strengths and how to best use them for the glory of God. Your niche is not just your area of expertise; it's a testament to God's grace and your unique place within His plan.

Remember, your platform is not just about you; it's about serving others and sharing the transformative power of faith. By carefully defining your niche, you're not just building a platform; you're building a ministry, a community, a vessel for God's love and grace to flow through to those who need it most. This purposeful focus allows for authentic connection and a stronger impact on the lives you touch. This deep connection built on mutual understanding and a shared faith allows you to bring hope and encouragement to those around you. The clearer your focus, the stronger your message and the greater your impact. It's in this focused ministry that you'll experience the greatest fulfillment, knowing you're using your gifts and talents to build God's kingdom. This intentional, strategic approach to building your platform is not just about success; it's about faithful service and obedience to God's calling in your life.

Networking and Collaboration

Having defined your niche and established the foundational elements of your platform, the next crucial step is to cultivate a network of supportive and collaborative relationships. This isn't simply about collecting business cards; it's about building genuine connections with individuals who share your passion for faith and your commitment to serving others. These relationships will become invaluable resources, opening doors to new opportunities and amplifying your message. Think of your network as a living, breathing organism, constantly growing and evolving, fueled by mutual support and shared purpose.

Networking, in the context of building a faith-based platform, transcends mere professional advancement. It's about fostering a community, a fellowship of believers working together to spread the Gospel and make a positive impact on the world. This involves actively seeking out opportunities to connect with like-minded individuals, whether through in-person events or online platforms. Attend conferences, workshops, and seminars related to your field.

These events provide invaluable opportunities to meet professionals, learn new skills, and gain exposure to different perspectives. Don't just attend these events passively; actively engage in conversations, share your experiences, and listen attentively to what others have to share.

Consider joining relevant online communities and forums. These digital spaces provide platforms to connect with people from all over the world who share your interests and values. Engage in discussions, offer helpful advice, and participate in meaningful conversations. Building an online presence, even a simple one, is crucial for connecting with potential collaborators and expanding your reach. Remember, your goal isn't merely to promote yourself, but to contribute meaningfully to the conversation and to help others. Genuine engagement, offering value to the community, is much more powerful than self-promotion.

Networking doesn't end with online communities; it extends to building relationships with potential clients and collaborators in your local area. This might involve attending local church events, participating in community initiatives, or volunteering your time and talents. These activities offer opportunities to connect with individuals who could benefit from your services or who might be able to support your platform. Be mindful of the relationships you're building, seeking to foster genuine connections rather than transactional interactions.

Collaboration is another vital component of building a strong platform. It involves working with other professionals and organizations to achieve shared goals. This could include co-hosting workshops, writing joint articles, or partnering on projects. Collaboration not only broadens your reach, but it also fosters creativity and innovation. By working with others, you can leverage your combined strengths to create something greater than you could achieve alone. Furthermore, collaboration strengthens your network, forging bonds of trust and mutual respect that can last for years. Consider potential collaborations with other authors, speakers, coaches, or organizations that align with your values and mission.

When seeking collaborative opportunities, look for individuals or organizations that complement your skills and expertise, rather than competing with them. A collaborative relationship should be mutually beneficial, with each party contributing unique strengths and gaining something valuable in return. Be prepared to give and receive, and ensure that your collaborative efforts are aligned with your overall goals and values. For example, if you're a life coach specializing in helping women overcome anxiety, you might collaborate with a Christian counselor who specializes in trauma recovery. This creates a synergy, allowing you to offer a more comprehensive range of support to your clients. Or, perhaps you're a writer who could partner with an artist to create inspiring devotional materials. The possibilities for collaboration are virtually limitless.

Successful collaborations are built on strong communication and mutual respect. Before embarking on any collaborative venture, clearly define roles, responsibilities, and expectations. This prevents misunderstandings and ensures that everyone is on the same page.

Establish clear communication channels and maintain regular contact to ensure that everyone is updated on progress and any potential challenges are addressed proactively. Develop a plan to handle conflicts fairly and respectfully, maintaining a focus on the shared goals. Remember, collaborations are not always easy, but the rewards are substantial. The combined expertise and expanded reach can exponentially impact your ability to serve others.

Throughout your networking efforts, remember the importance of reciprocity. Building relationships is a two-way street; offer value to others as you seek to receive value from them. Be genuinely interested in others' work, offer support and encouragement, and be willing to contribute to their success. This principle of giving freely and expecting nothing in return is deeply rooted in Christian teachings, and it's a powerful approach to relationship-building. This selfless service will build trust and respect, strengthening your network and opening doors to future collaborations.

Building your network and fostering collaborative partnerships requires time, effort, and commitment. It's not a quick fix; it's a long-term investment that yields significant returns. But the rewards are well worth the effort. As you expand your reach and influence through these connections, you'll find new opportunities to serve others, share your faith, and make a positive impact on the world. Consider your network as an extension of your ministry, a collective body working together to further the kingdom of God.

Remember the parable of the talents in Matthew 25:14-30. The master entrusted his servants with different talents, and each was expected to use those talents to produce a return. Your network and your collaborative partnerships are your talents; use them wisely, responsibly, and generously to amplify your impact and build God's kingdom. Don't hoard your connections; share them, use them, and watch as they become instruments of blessing for yourself and others. This generous approach creates a ripple effect, expanding your influence and deepening your faith.

Consider regularly reviewing your network and evaluating its effectiveness. Are you actively engaging with your contacts? Are your collaborations bearing fruit? Are you adding new connections while maintaining meaningful relationships with those already established? Periodically evaluate the strength of your connections, and consider strategies to nurture those relationships. Perhaps a simple email, a phone call, or a brief note of encouragement can strengthen those bonds.

Think strategically about the people you're surrounding yourself with. Are they encouraging your spiritual growth? Are they helping you stay accountable to your goals? Are they aligned with your values? Your network should be a source of support, encouragement, and accountability, helping you to stay focused on your mission and to overcome challenges. Choose to surround yourself with individuals who uplift you and inspire you to become the best version of yourself. This intentional cultivation of positive relationships will enhance your overall well-being and strengthen your platform.

Building a robust network and forging meaningful collaborations aren't just practical steps in building your platform; they are expressions of faith, reflecting a commitment to community and shared purpose. By actively seeking connections, offering support to others, and engaging in mutually beneficial collaborations, you are demonstrating the love and grace of Christ in tangible ways. Remember, your platform is a vessel for sharing God's message, and your connections are the pathways through which that message flows.

As you develop your platform, remember that it is not just a means to an end, but a journey of faith, a process of growth and transformation. Embrace the challenges, celebrate the victories, and always remember the importance of serving others with a humble and compassionate heart. As you build your platform, you are also building your character, strengthening your faith, and deepening your relationship with God. The rewards extend far beyond professional success; they touch the lives of others and contribute to the growth of God's kingdom. This process is a testament to your commitment to serving God through your talents, and it's in this faithful service that you find true fulfillment.

Content Creation and Marketing

Now that you've established a strong foundation for your platform and cultivated a supportive network, it's time to focus on the engine that drives its growth: consistent, high-quality content and a well-defined marketing strategy. This isn't about creating a flood of mediocre material; it's about strategically crafting messages that resonate deeply with your target audience and align perfectly with your Christian values and your unique niche. Think of your content as seeds of faith, carefully planted and nurtured to bear fruit in the lives of others.

The first step in this process is developing a content calendar. This isn't a rigid, inflexible schedule, but rather a flexible roadmap guiding your content creation. Consider your niche; what specific needs and questions does your target audience have? Are you focusing on marriage and family, overcoming addiction, navigating workplace challenges from a faith-based perspective, or perhaps offering spiritual guidance for young adults? Tailor your content to directly address these needs, providing practical advice, inspirational stories, and insightful reflections grounded in biblical principles.

For instance, if your niche is focused on supporting Christian women entrepreneurs, your content could include blog posts on balancing faith and business, podcasts featuring interviews with successful Christian female business owners, or even online courses teaching practical business skills from a faith-based perspective. Similarly, if your focus is on fostering stronger family relationships, your content might consist of blog posts on effective communication techniques within families, videos offering practical tips for family devotions, or online workshops focused on conflict resolution rooted in Christian values.

The key is consistency. Regularly publishing new and engaging content keeps your audience returning for more. A consistent publishing schedule also tells search engines that your platform is active and relevant, improving your search engine optimization (SEO). Experiment with various content formats – blog posts, videos, podcasts, infographics, social media updates – to appeal to a broader audience and keep your content fresh and engaging.

Analyze the performance of your content to understand what resonates best with your audience. What pieces generate the most engagement? Which platforms are yielding the highest conversion rates? Use this data to inform future content creation and refine your overall strategy.

Remember that your content should always be authentic and reflective of your personal faith journey. Don't try to be someone you're not; instead, let your genuine passion and unwavering faith shine through in every piece you create. Authenticity breeds trust, and trust is the foundation of any successful platform. This isn't about crafting a flawless, polished image; it's about sharing your experiences, your struggles, and your triumphs, allowing your vulnerability to connect you with your audience on a deeper level. Let your writing reflect the compassion and grace of Christ.

Once your content is created, you need an effective marketing strategy to reach your target audience. This involves more than just posting on social media; it's about developing a comprehensive plan that integrates various methods to maximize your reach and impact.

Start by identifying the platforms where your target audience is most active. Are they primarily on Instagram, Facebook, Twitter, or perhaps Pinterest or YouTube? Focus your efforts on these platforms, tailoring your content and messaging to each one.

Each platform requires a unique approach. Instagram thrives on visual content, so high-quality images and videos are crucial. Facebook allows for longer-form posts and engagement through groups and communities. Twitter demands brevity and quick, impactful messaging. Utilize the unique strengths of each platform to your advantage. Consider paid advertising. While organic reach is important, targeted advertising campaigns on platforms like

Facebook and Instagram can significantly expand your reach and help you connect with individuals who might not otherwise discover your platform. Analyze your ad campaigns to optimize your spending and ensure that your message is resonating with the right audience.

Beyond paid advertising, explore other promotional strategies such as guest blogging on relevant websites, collaborating with other Christian influencers in your niche, participating in online and offline events, and engaging actively in relevant online communities. These collaborations help you build relationships, broaden your reach, and expose your platform to a wider audience. When collaborating with others, ensure that the collaboration aligns with your values and the overall message you're seeking to convey. This ensures a consistent and authentic brand identity.

Another crucial aspect of marketing is email marketing. Building an email list provides a direct line of communication with your audience, allowing you to share updates, promote new content, and foster deeper connections. Offer valuable content, such as free ebooks or webinars, as incentives for people to join your email list. Always respect your subscribers' privacy and provide them with high-quality, relevant content that strengthens your relationship with them. Finally, don't underestimate the power of word-of-mouth marketing. Encourage your audience to share your content and engage with your platform. Respond to comments and messages promptly, showing your appreciation for their support. Build a community around your platform where people feel valued and connected.

Word-of-mouth referrals are invaluable because they come from trusted sources, and this type of authentic endorsement strengthens your brand and builds credibility.

Remember that building a successful platform takes time, patience, and perseverance. Don't get discouraged if you don't see results overnight. Consistent effort, a well-defined strategy, and a heart dedicated to serving others are the keys to creating a platform that glorifies God and makes a positive impact on the lives of your audience. Each piece of content, each interaction, each connection—all contribute to the larger picture of your ministry's growth and expansion. It's a journey of faith, a testament to your commitment, and a reflection of God's grace working in and through your life.

Trust in His timing, embrace the challenges, and celebrate the victories along the way. Above all, remember to pray for guidance and wisdom as you continue to build your platform and share your message with the world. Your work is a reflection of your faith, and in that, you find profound meaning and purpose. As you diligently craft your content and thoughtfully employ your marketing strategies, remember that your ultimate goal is not simply to amass followers or achieve online success; it's to serve God and impact the lives of others for His glory. Let your faith be the compass that guides you, ensuring that every aspect of your platform aligns with your spiritual values and contributes to the growth of God's Kingdom. The rewards of this dedicated service extend far beyond any measure of online success; they reach into the hearts and lives of others, leaving a lasting legacy of faith and hope.

Managing Expectations and Avoiding Burnout

The exhilaration of building a platform for your ministry can be intoxicating. Witnessing the growth of your online community, feeling the impact of your message resonating with others, it's easy to get caught up in the momentum. However, this relentless pursuit of progress can quickly lead to burnout if not carefully managed. This is not a sign of weakness, but a crucial aspect of maintaining long-term sustainability and ensuring your work is a testament to your faith and not a source of exhaustion. The key is to cultivate a balanced approach, integrating intentional self-care practices into your daily routine. This isn't about self-indulgence; it's about recognizing the vital importance of replenishing your spiritual, mental, and physical resources, allowing you to serve effectively and remain true to your calling.

The first step in avoiding burnout is to establish healthy boundaries. This involves defining clear limits on your work hours, your online engagement, and your overall commitment. Many of us struggle with the always-on culture of the digital age, feeling an unrelenting pressure to respond to messages, create content, and stay connected twenty-four-seven. This constant connectivity can blur the lines between work and personal life, leading to feelings of overwhelm and exhaustion. Actively choosing when to disconnect—to step away from your computer, to silence notifications, to prioritize offline activities—is not a sign of laziness but a strategic act of self-preservation. Think of it as a form of spiritual discipline, a way of safeguarding your time and energy for the tasks that truly matter, both in your ministry and in your personal life.

Implementing these boundaries may require saying "no" to opportunities that don't align with your priorities or stretch your resources too thin. This can feel uncomfortable initially, but it's essential for protecting your well-being. Remember that your platform is a means to an end, not an end in itself. Your ultimate goal is to serve God and impact others; a depleted and burned-out you cannot effectively fulfill that calling. Learning to prioritize tasks and delegate responsibilities where possible is another crucial aspect of boundary setting. Can certain tasks be outsourced? Are there volunteers who could assist you with specific projects?

Identifying areas where you can lessen your workload allows you to concentrate your energy on the most critical aspects of your ministry. Managing expectations is equally vital in preventing burnout. It's tempting to compare your progress to others, falling into the trap of measuring success solely by the number of followers, likes, or comments. This comparison game can be incredibly draining and disheartening, leading to feelings of inadequacy and frustration.

Remember that everyone's journey is unique, and God's timing is perfect. Focus on your own progress, celebrating the small victories and learning from the challenges along the way. Instead of fixating on external validation, cultivate a deep sense of inner peace and fulfillment derived from your dedication to serving God and your community.

Prioritize self-care as a spiritual discipline. This encompasses various aspects of your well-being, including physical, emotional, and spiritual renewal. Physical self-care involves engaging in regular exercise, maintaining a healthy diet, and ensuring adequate sleep. These may seem like mundane aspects of life, but they form the bedrock of your physical resilience and energy levels.

Neglecting your physical health will inevitably impact your emotional and spiritual well-being. Just as a car needs fuel and maintenance to run efficiently, your body requires nourishment and rest to function optimally. Incorporate physical activity into your daily routine, even if it's just a short walk or a brief exercise session. Nourish your body with wholesome, nutritious foods that provide the energy you need to sustain your work. And prioritize sleep, allowing your body and mind to rest and rejuvenate.

Emotional self-care involves managing stress and maintaining healthy relationships. This includes actively practicing techniques like mindfulness, meditation, or journaling to help manage stress and anxiety. It also involves cultivating strong, supportive relationships with family, friends, and fellow believers. Sharing your burdens and celebrating your triumphs with others can significantly impact your overall emotional well-being. Recognize the importance of connecting with others who understand your journey and can provide encouragement and support. A strong network of like-minded individuals can provide a vital source of strength and resilience during challenging times. Don't underestimate the power of community; it's a vital component of both your personal and professional well-being.

Spiritual self-care is arguably the most crucial aspect of preventing burnout, particularly for Christian ministry leaders. This involves spending dedicated time in prayer, Bible study, and worship. This isn't merely a checklist of religious duties; it's a vital means of replenishing your spiritual reserves and reconnecting with God's presence and guidance. Regular time spent in prayer allows you to seek God's wisdom and direction, providing you with the strength and clarity to navigate the challenges of building your platform. Bible study nourishes your soul, reminding you of God's unwavering love, faithfulness, and provision. And worship helps you connect with God on a deeper level, experiencing the joy and peace that only He can provide. Remember that your ministry is a spiritual endeavor; therefore, your spiritual well-being is paramount to its success.

Remember that avoiding burnout is not about achieving perfection; it's about pursuing a sustainable and balanced approach to your ministry. It's about recognizing your limitations, setting healthy boundaries, prioritizing self-care, and trusting in God's guidance.

This involves regularly evaluating your schedule, your workload, and your overall well-being. Are you feeling overwhelmed? Are you neglecting important areas of your life? If so, it's time to make adjustments. Don't wait until you're completely depleted before addressing the issue. Regular self-assessment is key to preventing burnout and maintaining long-term effectiveness in your ministry.

It's also vital to celebrate your successes and acknowledge your achievements along the way. It's easy to focus solely on what still needs to be done, neglecting to appreciate the progress you've already made. Take time to reflect on your accomplishments, both large and small, and give thanks to God for His blessings. This is not self-congratulation but a healthy recognition of God's work in your life and a way to reaffirm your dedication to your ministry.

Celebrating milestones, whether it's reaching a certain number of followers, launching a new project, or receiving positive feedback from your audience, helps you maintain a positive outlook and prevents feelings of discouragement.

Ultimately, building a successful platform for your Christian ministry is a marathon, not a sprint. Maintaining a balanced approach, prioritizing self-care, and managing your expectations are crucial for long-term sustainability and effectiveness. Remember that your well-being is not a luxury; it's a necessity. By taking care of yourself, both spiritually and physically, you'll be better equipped to serve God and impact the lives of others for His glory.

The journey may be challenging, but with God's grace and guidance, you can build a platform that not only glorifies Him but also sustains you in the process. Embrace the journey, trust His timing, and remember that true success lies in faithfulness and unwavering dedication to His calling. Your platform, however successful, is a tool to serve, not a measure of your worth. This perspective protects you from the insidious pressures of online performance and allows you to center your focus where it truly matters: your relationship with God and your service to others.

Biblical Examples of Influence

The previous section emphasized the importance of self-care and sustainable practices in building a ministry platform. Now, let's turn our attention to the rich tapestry of biblical examples that illuminate the path toward effective and God-honoring influence.

Examining the lives of influential figures in scripture offers invaluable insights into strategies, approaches, and the crucial role of faith in shaping impactful ministries.

Consider Moses, a man initially hesitant and self-doubting, yet chosen by God to lead His people out of slavery. Moses's platform wasn't built overnight; it was forged in the fires of his own struggles and God's relentless refining. His influence stemmed not from self-promotion but from unwavering obedience to God's commands. His leadership, though demanding and challenging, was rooted in a deep relationship with God, enabling him to guide and inspire millions. His reliance on God's strength, even when facing Pharaoh's relentless opposition, serves as a powerful lesson in humility and dependence. The parting of the Red Sea, the provision of manna in the desert, and the giving of the Law at Sinai—these weren't merely historical events; they were demonstrations of God's power channeled through Moses's faithfulness. The effectiveness of his platform was directly proportional to his reliance on God's guidance and his unwavering commitment to His purpose. He didn't seek popularity or personal gain; his platform was entirely focused on God's glory and the liberation of His people. This focus prevented the potential pitfalls of pride and self-aggrandizement that often plague those who build a large following. His story reminds us that true influence flows from a deep wellspring of spiritual connection, not from self-promotion or manipulation.

Another potent example is the prophet Nehemiah, whose influence wasn't built on charisma or oratory skill, but on unwavering dedication and fervent prayer. Faced with the daunting task of rebuilding Jerusalem's walls, Nehemiah didn't rely solely on his own strength or political acumen. His platform was built on a foundation of prayer and unwavering reliance on God. His strategy was carefully planned, involving meticulous organization, resource management, and the galvanization of the community. He didn't just oversee the physical reconstruction; he also revitalized the spiritual life of the community, fostering a sense of unity and shared purpose. This holistic approach demonstrates the importance of considering all aspects of building a ministry platform—spiritual, logistical, and interpersonal. His willingness to confront opposition, his steadfast commitment, and his unwavering faith in God's power made him an exceptionally effective leader. His success wasn't measured solely by the completed walls, but by the renewed spirit of a community restored through faith and collaborative effort. This underscores the vital role of community in building a lasting platform for ministry. Nehemiah's example teaches us that effective leadership often requires difficult conversations, decisive actions, and the courage to stand firm in the face of adversity.

The Apostle Paul, a transformative figure in early Christianity, presents a powerful case study in strategic influence. His ministry wasn't confined to a single location; he traveled extensively, establishing churches and spreading the Gospel throughout the Roman Empire. He understood the importance of adapting his message to diverse audiences, demonstrating remarkable adaptability and cultural sensitivity. Paul's platform was built on tireless evangelism, effective communication, and the establishment of strong leadership within the early Christian communities. He didn't shy away from confronting opposition or facing persecution; instead, he used these experiences to further strengthen his message and solidify his commitment to his calling. He masterfully utilized both personal interactions and written communication, establishing a powerful and lasting influence that continues to shape Christianity today. His epistles, carefully crafted letters to various churches, became foundational texts for Christian doctrine and practice. He employed a multi-faceted approach, using both formal and informal methods to spread the Gospel. His ability to connect with diverse audiences and adapt his message effectively demonstrates the importance of understanding context and audience engagement in building a ministry platform. The power of his words, coupled with his unwavering faith, allowed him to transcend cultural and social barriers.

Unlike modern platforms driven by algorithmic engagement, these biblical examples emphasize authenticity, community, and unwavering faith as essential pillars. Paul's travels, Moses's leadership, and Nehemiah's rebuilding project weren't driven by social media metrics or fleeting trends, but by a deep commitment to God's purpose. Their effectiveness wasn't measured in follower counts or website traffic, but in the lasting impact on individuals and communities. This perspective shift is critical for anyone seeking to build a ministry platform that truly honors God. It is about impact, not impressions.

Another often-overlooked aspect of building influence is the quiet, consistent service exemplified by individuals like Dorcas, mentioned in Acts 9:36-42. Dorcas wasn't a charismatic preacher or a prominent leader; her platform was built on acts of kindness and compassion. Her influence stemmed from her consistent, selfless service to others, a legacy that transcended her earthly life and is still remembered and celebrated centuries later. Her story reminds us that influence isn't always about grand gestures or public pronouncements; it can also be found in the quiet acts of service, the unnoticed deeds of love and compassion, which often have a profound and lasting impact on those around us. It's a reminder that even seemingly small acts of service, consistently performed with love, can create a ripple effect of positive influence. Her story challenges us to re-evaluate our definition of "platform" and consider the subtle yet powerful ways we can make a difference. It shows that influence is not always about being seen; it's often about being present, loving, and serving.

The women of Proverbs 31 provide a compelling example of influence through practical wisdom and hard work. Their platform wasn't built on fame or fortune, but on diligent work and unwavering commitment to their families and communities. Their influence stemmed from their character, their leadership within the home, and their quiet yet powerful contributions to society. They exemplify the concept that genuine influence is built through integrity, diligence, and a commitment to service. Their lives serve as a powerful reminder that influence is not solely about the grand stage or the massive audience but also about quietly and consistently living a life that reflects faith and inspires others. Their actions demonstrate that influence can be found in the everyday, in the mundane and the meticulous tasks of life.

These biblical examples offer a comprehensive understanding of the principles involved in building a platform for ministry. Their stories highlight the crucial role of faith, perseverance, and reliance on God's guidance in achieving lasting and meaningful impact. They show that influence is not primarily about self-promotion but about serving others and fulfilling God's calling. The methods may differ—from Moses's leadership to Dorcas's kindness, from Nehemiah's reconstruction project to Paul's missionary journeys—but the underlying principle remains consistent: genuine influence stems from a life lived in service to God and a heart dedicated to His purpose. These examples serve not as blueprints to be copied, but as inspiring narratives to guide us in discerning God's purpose for our own lives and platforms.

Moving forward, remember that your platform is a tool for God's purpose, not a measure of your self-worth. The effectiveness of your platform is directly proportional to your faithfulness to God, your commitment to His calling, and your dedication to serving others. Let these biblical examples guide you as you build your platform, ensuring that your influence is a testament to God's grace and a beacon of His love to the world. The pursuit of a larger audience should never overshadow the more important goal of impacting individual lives for His glory. Instead of focusing on the size of your platform, focus on the depth of your relationship with God and the authenticity of your message. This is where true and lasting influence is born, and from which you will derive a lasting sense of fulfillment in ministry. The principles highlighted in these biblical examples—

faith, perseverance, humility, community, and service—will sustain you through the inevitable challenges and help you build a platform that is both impactful and enduring, glorifying God in all you do. May your platform reflect the heart of Christ, and become a vehicle for His transforming love to reach a world in desperate need of hope and healing.

Setting Goals and Tracking Progress

Building a sustainable ministry platform, as discussed previously, requires more than just passion and prayer; it demands strategic planning and consistent effort. Having established a foundation rooted in self-care and inspired by biblical examples, we now shift our focus to the crucial aspect of goal setting and progress tracking.

This is not merely about ticking boxes on a to-do list; it's about fostering a mindset of continuous growth and refinement, ensuring that your ministry efforts remain aligned with God's purpose and your individual calling. Think of it as charting a course across the ocean of ministry – you need a destination in mind (your goals) and a method for checking your position regularly (progress tracking). Without these tools, you risk drifting aimlessly, losing momentum and becoming disheartened.

The process of setting goals for your ministry platform should be deeply prayerful. Begin by seeking God's guidance. What are His specific intentions for your life and ministry? What unique gifts and talents has He bestowed upon you? These are crucial questions to contemplate. Avoid setting goals based solely on what you see others achieving. Your path is unique, tailored by God for your specific calling. Instead, focus on identifying areas where your skills and passions intersect with the needs of your community and the overarching purpose of spreading the Gospel.

Once you've sought divine direction, begin crafting SMART goals. This acronym—Specific, Measurable, Achievable, Relevant, and Time-bound—provides a framework for ensuring your goals are clear, focused, and realistic. A vague goal like "grow my online presence" is unhelpful. Instead, a SMART goal might be: "Increase my Instagram following by 1000 followers within the next three months by posting consistently engaging content, interacting with followers, and utilizing relevant hashtags." Notice how this goal is specific, measurable, achievable, relevant to your ministry's objectives, and bound by a timeframe.

The "achievable" aspect is particularly important. While ambition is admirable, setting overly ambitious goals can lead to discouragement and burnout. Begin with smaller, more manageable goals that you can realistically achieve. Success breeds success. As you achieve these initial goals, you'll build momentum, confidence, and a strong foundation upon which to build larger, more ambitious goals. This gradual progression is crucial for maintaining long-term commitment and preventing feelings of overwhelm.

Alongside setting goals, the creation of a robust system for tracking progress is paramount. This might involve utilizing a simple spreadsheet, a dedicated project management app, or even a good old-fashioned notebook. The key is consistency. Regularly record your progress toward each goal, noting both successes and setbacks.

This process provides valuable insights into your effectiveness, identifies areas needing improvement, and helps you remain accountable to yourself and, ultimately, to God. Consider scheduling regular times for review and reflection – perhaps a weekly or monthly meeting with a trusted mentor or accountability partner.

Don't shy away from celebrating your milestones. Acknowledging your achievements, both big and small, helps to reinforce positive habits and maintain motivation. Remember, ministry is a marathon, not a sprint. There will be times of rapid progress, and there will be times of slower growth. Celebrate the victories and learn from the setbacks. This balanced approach prevents discouragement and fosters a spirit of resilience. Even seemingly small accomplishments contribute to the overall progress and should be acknowledged. A single soul touched by your ministry is a significant achievement that deserves recognition and gratitude.

Regular review and adjustment are critical components of maintaining momentum. Your goals should not be static; they should evolve as your ministry grows and your understanding of God's purpose deepens. Periodically reassess your goals, asking yourself: Are these goals still aligned with God's calling? Are they still relevant to the needs of my community? Are they still achievable given my current resources and capabilities? If the answer to any of these questions is no, don't hesitate to adjust your goals accordingly. Flexibility and adaptability are essential traits for navigating the ever-changing landscape of ministry.

The process of tracking progress also reveals opportunities for improvement. By analyzing your results, you can identify strategies that are working well and those that need refinement. Perhaps a particular social media platform isn't yielding the desired results, or a specific type of content isn't resonating with your audience. These insights provide valuable opportunities for course correction, allowing you to optimize your efforts and maximize your impact. Remember, data-driven decision-making is not about replacing prayer and intuition, but augmenting them with objective information.

Another crucial aspect of goal setting and progress tracking is the element of accountability. Sharing your goals and progress with a trusted mentor, spiritual advisor, or accountability partner can significantly enhance your chances of success. This individual can provide support, encouragement, and constructive feedback, helping you stay focused and motivated. They can also offer fresh perspectives and challenge you to consider alternative approaches. Accountability isn't about judgment; it's about mutual support and encouragement in the pursuit of God's purpose.

Moreover, the process of setting goals and tracking progress should be a reflective one. It is a time to seek God's wisdom and guidance, not just to review statistics. Reflect on your experiences, both positive and negative. What did you learn from your successes?

What adjustments can you make to overcome challenges? This introspective approach helps integrate your ministry with your personal spiritual journey, ensuring that your efforts are not just outwardly focused but also deeply rooted in a growing relationship with God.

The goal-setting and progress-tracking system you develop should be personalized to your individual needs and circumstances. What works for one individual might not work for another. Experiment with different methods until you find a system that suits your personality, your ministry's specific needs, and, most importantly, your spiritual journey. Remember, this is a process of spiritual growth and refinement, not a rigid formula. The flexibility and adaptability you display in this process will serve you well as you navigate the ongoing journey of ministry.

Ultimately, the aim is not to achieve a certain number of followers, likes, or views, but to effectively and faithfully serve God. Numbers can be indicative of progress, but they should never overshadow the deeper purpose of your ministry – to spread the Gospel, build community, and share God's love with the world. Remember to pray regularly for guidance, wisdom, and perseverance. Trust in God's plan for your life and ministry, and allow your faith to fuel your commitment to achieving your goals, always keeping in mind that His glory is the ultimate reward. The journey of building a God-honoring platform is an ongoing process of learning, growth, and refinement—a continuous reflection of your deepening relationship with Him. Embrace the journey, trust His timing, and watch as He uses your dedication and perseverance to achieve His glorious purpose.

Adapting to Change
and Challenges

The unwavering commitment we've discussed to building a God-honoring ministry platform requires not only strategic planning and consistent effort, but also an unwavering spirit of adaptability. The path of ministry, much like life itself, is rarely a straight line.

Unexpected challenges, unforeseen obstacles, and even outright setbacks are inevitable. How we respond to these difficulties will determine whether we maintain momentum or falter under pressure. The key lies in cultivating resilience and adaptability – a willingness to bend, but not break, in the face of adversity. This isn't about avoiding challenges, but rather about navigating them with faith, wisdom, and a proactive approach.

Think of the biblical examples of resilience. Joseph, sold into slavery and falsely accused, ultimately rose to a position of power in Egypt, saving his family from famine. David, a shepherd boy, faced Goliath and, through faith and courage, overcame seemingly insurmountable odds. These stories aren't just historical accounts; they are blueprints for navigating our own challenges. They remind us that even in the darkest of times, God's hand is at work, shaping us, strengthening us, and preparing us for greater things.

Adaptability, in the context of ministry, translates to flexibility in our strategies, our methods, and even our expectations. What worked last year might not work this year. A ministry initiative that thrived in one community might struggle in another. We must be willing to adjust our approach, to learn from our mistakes, and to embrace change as an opportunity for growth. Rigid adherence to a pre-conceived plan, without the flexibility to adapt to changing circumstances, can lead to stagnation and ultimately, failure. It's about being sensitive to the Spirit's leading, recognizing when adjustments are needed, and having the courage to make those changes.

Developing this adaptability isn't a passive process. It requires conscious effort, intentional practice, and a willingness to step outside of our comfort zones. This includes developing robust problem-solving skills. When faced with a challenge, resist the urge to panic or become discouraged. Instead, approach the situation with prayerful reflection and careful consideration. Ask yourself: What is the root cause of the problem? What resources do I have available to me? Who can I consult for advice and support? What are potential solutions, and which one aligns best with God's leading?

Remember the importance of seeking counsel from trusted mentors and fellow ministers. Sharing our burdens and seeking guidance from those who have walked similar paths can provide invaluable perspective and support. They can offer insights we might have overlooked, provide encouragement when we feel disheartened, and remind us of God's unwavering presence even amidst the storm. These relationships are crucial in maintaining momentum through challenging times; they offer a lifeline of support and a platform for shared learning.

Furthermore, developing resilience means viewing setbacks as opportunities for growth and learning. Failure is not the opposite of success; it's a stepping stone towards it. Every challenge, every obstacle, every setback, provides valuable lessons that can shape us and strengthen our ministry. Don't dwell on past mistakes, but analyze them dispassionately to identify areas for improvement. What did you learn from this experience? How can you apply those lessons to future endeavors? This mindset of continuous learning and refinement is crucial for maintaining momentum in the long term.

Consider the example of a pastor who planned a large-scale community outreach event, only to have it poorly attended. Instead of viewing this as a failure, he could analyze the factors that contributed to the low turnout. Perhaps the promotion was inadequate, the timing inconvenient, or the event itself not effectively targeted to the community's needs. By carefully evaluating these factors, he could learn valuable lessons about event planning and marketing, making future events more successful. This proactive approach transforms potential setbacks into opportunities for future growth and refinement.

Flexibility is also key in navigating unforeseen obstacles. Life rarely follows a neat, predictable plan. Unexpected events, personal crises, and external circumstances can disrupt even the most meticulously crafted ministry plans. In such moments, it's crucial to maintain a sense of calm and to adapt to the changing landscape. This might involve adjusting timelines, revising strategies, or even completely re-evaluating the direction of a particular project. The willingness to adjust and refocus is a testament to our faith in God's plan, even when that plan looks different than we anticipated.

Consider a ministry that planned a series of workshops on spiritual growth, but due to an unexpected pandemic, was forced to transition to an entirely online format. This required adapting their methods, learning new technologies, and overcoming the challenges of engaging an audience online. However, by remaining flexible and adapting to the circumstances, they were able to continue their ministry and even reach a wider audience than originally anticipated. This demonstrates the importance of embracing change and finding creative solutions in the face of adversity.

Another crucial aspect of adapting to change and challenges lies in fostering a strong sense of self-care. The demands of ministry can be significant, both emotionally and mentally. Burnout is a real threat, and it can severely impact our ability to maintain momentum.

Prioritizing self-care—getting adequate rest, engaging in healthy activities, spending time in prayer and meditation—is not selfish; it's essential for sustaining long-term ministry effectiveness. This is not about self-indulgence, but about replenishing our spiritual and emotional resources, so that we can continue to serve God effectively.

Regular prayer and meditation are vital tools in navigating challenges. They provide a source of strength, guidance, and peace in the midst of difficult circumstances. Through prayer, we connect with God, seeking His wisdom and guidance in making decisions and overcoming obstacles. Meditation allows us to center ourselves, to quiet the noise of the world, and to listen to the still, small voice of the Spirit. These practices are essential for maintaining emotional and spiritual equilibrium, enabling us to respond to challenges with faith, grace, and wisdom.

Finally, remember the importance of celebrating small victories along the way. Focusing solely on the ultimate goal can be discouraging, especially when faced with significant challenges. Celebrating small achievements helps to maintain momentum and reinforces a positive outlook. It's about acknowledging progress, no matter how small, and giving thanks to God for His guidance and support. This positive reinforcement strengthens our resolve and motivates us to continue pressing forward. Every step forward, every obstacle overcome, is a testament to God's faithfulness and a cause for celebration. The journey is long, but the rewards are worth the effort. The journey of ministry, filled with its inevitable challenges and changes, is a journey of continuous growth, refinement, and deepening faith. Embrace the journey, trust in God's plan, and watch Him work through you to achieve His magnificent purposes.

Prioritizing Self-Care and Rest

The relentless pursuit of building a God-honoring ministry platform, as we've explored, demands not only strategic planning and consistent effort but also a profound commitment to self-care. It's a counter-intuitive truth: the more we pour ourselves out in service, the more crucial it becomes to replenish our own spiritual, mental, and physical reserves. Neglecting self-care isn't simply unwise; it's a recipe for burnout, frustration, and ultimately, a diminished capacity to serve effectively. Think of it like this: a car needs fuel to run. Similarly, you need self-care to sustain your ministry journey.

This isn't about self-indulgence or prioritizing personal comfort above the needs of others. Rather, self-care is a vital act of stewardship, a recognition that God has entrusted you with a precious gift – yourself – and that taking care of this gift is essential for fulfilling His purpose. It's about recognizing your limitations, understanding your boundaries, and proactively implementing strategies that ensure your long-term sustainability and effectiveness. Without this essential element, the momentum you've worked so hard to build will inevitably falter. The well runs dry if it's not replenished. Let's delve deeper into the practical aspects of incorporating self-care into your ministry life. First, consider your physical well-being.

This isn't merely about avoiding illness; it's about cultivating a vibrant, healthy body that's capable of withstanding the demands of ministry. Regular exercise, even in small increments, is crucial. A brisk walk, a short deep breathing session, or a simple set of stretches can do wonders for both your physical and mental health. Find activities you genuinely enjoy and incorporate them into your routine, treating them as non-negotiable appointments. Remember, you're not just serving others; you're serving God, and He deserves your best.

Equally important is the quality of your sleep. Adequate rest is not a luxury; it's a necessity. Aim for seven to eight hours of uninterrupted sleep each night. Create a relaxing bedtime routine that helps your mind and body wind down. This might include a warm bath, reading a spiritually uplifting book, or simply spending quiet time in prayer and reflection. Chronic sleep deprivation significantly impacts cognitive function, emotional regulation, and overall well-being, hindering your ability to effectively minister to others. Prioritize sleep as an investment in your ability to serve. Consider it a spiritual discipline.

Nutrition plays a significant role as well. Fuel your body with wholesome, nourishing foods. Avoid excessive sugar, processed foods, and caffeine, which can lead to energy crashes and mood swings. Instead, opt for a balanced diet rich in fruits, vegetables, and lean protein. This doesn't have to be complicated; even small changes, like adding a salad to your lunch or swapping sugary drinks for water, can make a noticeable difference. Remember, the food you consume impacts not only your physical health but also your mental clarity and emotional stability. This is directly connected to your ability to effectively serve God and others.

Beyond the physical, self-care also encompasses your mental and emotional well-being. This involves actively managing stress, cultivating positive coping mechanisms, and seeking support when needed. Engage in activities that bring you joy and peace, whether it's spending time in nature, listening to music, reading, engaging in a hobby, or pursuing a creative outlet. These activities are not frivolous distractions; they are essential for maintaining a healthy mental and emotional balance. They refresh your spirit and help you to approach your ministry with renewed energy and focus.

The spiritual dimension of self-care is arguably the most crucial. This involves nurturing your relationship with God through consistent prayer, Bible study, and worship. Set aside dedicated time each day for spiritual practices. Even a few minutes of quiet reflection can make a profound difference in your overall well-being. This time allows you to connect with your source of strength, renew your spirit, and gain clarity and perspective. It's a time to receive guidance and direction for the challenges you face. It's an essential component to prevent burnout and maintain a consistent focus on your calling.

Consider incorporating spiritual practices like meditation, mindfulness, or journaling into your routine. These can help you to quiet the noise of the world, center yourself in God's presence, and gain a fresh perspective on challenges. Remember, your ministry is not solely about outward actions; it's deeply rooted in your inward spiritual life. Nurturing your relationship with God through these practices is fundamental to your ability to minister effectively and remain spiritually grounded.

Crucially, building a strong support network is essential. This involves surrounding yourself with people who understand your ministry and provide encouragement, accountability, and support. Share your burdens with trusted friends, family members, or mentors who can offer prayer, advice, and practical assistance.

Don't be afraid to ask for help when you need it. Remember, seeking support isn't a sign of weakness; it's a sign of wisdom and maturity. Isolation is a breeding ground for burnout and disillusionment. Choose community.

Finally, learn to set healthy boundaries. This is a crucial aspect of self-care often overlooked. Setting boundaries means learning to say "no" to commitments that will overextend you or compromise your well-being. It means protecting your time and energy for those activities that are most important, both for your ministry and your personal life. It's about recognizing your limitations and respecting your need for rest and rejuvenation. This isn't selfish; it's essential for long-term effectiveness. The ability to set boundaries demonstrates respect for yourself and for your commitment to the work God has called you to do. This is not about being unavailable, but about being strategically available.

In conclusion, maintaining momentum in your God-honoring ministry platform requires a holistic approach to self-care. It's a proactive investment in your physical, mental, emotional, and spiritual well-being, ensuring your long-term effectiveness and preventing burnout. Prioritize regular physical activity, adequate rest, a healthy diet, stress management techniques, spiritual disciplines, a strong support network, and healthy boundaries.

Remember, self-care isn't selfish; it's an act of obedience, a recognition of the precious gift God has given you, and a crucial component of your journey of faith and service. Your well-being is not merely personal; it is essential to the fulfillment of God's calling on your life. Embrace self-care as a spiritual discipline, and watch as it strengthens your ability to serve and bless others for His glory. The sustainable ministry is one built on a foundation of well-being, fueled by faith, and powered by a heart surrendered to God's purposes.

Seeking Accountability and Support

The journey of building a God-honoring ministry platform is rarely a solitary one. While personal dedication and self-care are crucial, as we've discussed, they are most effective when complemented by a strong network of accountability and support. This isn't about weakness; it's about wisdom, recognizing the inherent limitations of attempting such a significant undertaking alone. The Apostle Paul himself relied on the support of fellow believers, highlighting the vital role of community in the Christian life. He frequently mentions his companions in his epistles, showcasing the power of collaborative ministry.

Think of your accountability partners as your spiritual cheerleaders and mentors, individuals who will celebrate your victories and gently guide you through setbacks. They are not there to judge or criticize, but to offer constructive feedback, encouragement, and prayer. The right accountability partners understand the unique challenges of ministry work and offer a safe space for vulnerability and honest self-assessment. They'll help you stay grounded in your faith, particularly when facing discouragement or temptation to stray from your divinely appointed path.

Choosing the right accountability partners is crucial. Look for individuals who possess a genuine love for God, a commitment to prayer, and a proven track record of faithfulness. They should be people who can offer wise counsel based on biblical principles, challenge you to grow spiritually, and hold you accountable to your commitments without being overly critical or judgmental. Their support should be constructive, fostering growth and encouraging perseverance, rather than fostering comparison or competition.

Consider the diverse roles accountability partners can play. Some might focus on prayer support, consistently interceding for your ministry's success and your personal well-being. Others could provide strategic counsel, offering valuable insights based on their own experiences or expertise. Still others might serve as a sounding board, offering a safe space to process your thoughts and feelings without judgment, helping you discern God's will for your ministry. The ideal team will offer a blend of these crucial support roles, ensuring a holistic approach to accountability.

Building a robust support network extends beyond accountability partners. It encompasses a wider circle of fellow believers who offer encouragement, prayer, and practical assistance. This could include mentors, peers in ministry, members of your church community, or even family and friends who understand and support your calling. This wider network provides emotional support, practical help, and a sense of belonging that is essential for long-term ministry effectiveness. It's a reminder that you're not alone in this journey, that there are others who believe in your vision and are committed to praying for its success.

The practical aspects of building a support network should not be overlooked. Consider actively engaging in fellowship opportunities within your church or local Christian community. Attend events, participate in small groups, and seek out mentors who have experience in ministry. Attend conferences or workshops that offer networking opportunities. Don't be afraid to reach out to those you admire, expressing your desire to learn from their experience and grow together. Remember, genuine relationships are built on mutual respect, trust, and shared commitment to God's work. It's a two-way street; you should offer the same level of support to others that you receive from them.

Shared accountability within your support network can be a powerful tool for maintaining momentum. Regular check-ins with your accountability partners can keep you on track with your goals, ensuring that you stay focused and avoid distractions. These check-ins should not be merely reporting sessions, but opportunities for prayer, encouragement, and honest self-reflection. Share your successes and struggles openly, allowing your partners to provide guidance and support as needed. This transparent approach fosters trust and strengthens the bonds of your support network.

One practical way to implement shared accountability is through regular meetings, either in person or via video call. During these meetings, discuss your progress towards your goals, address any challenges you've encountered, and seek advice and encouragement. Consider establishing a clear set of goals and milestones for your ministry platform, sharing these with your accountability partners and regularly reviewing your progress. This structured approach ensures that you stay focused and motivated, preventing procrastination and promoting consistent growth.

Remember that accountability is not about shame or criticism; it's about mutual support and encouragement. Create a safe space where everyone feels comfortable sharing their struggles and celebrating their victories. Emphasize prayer and mutual encouragement, fostering a spirit of love and unity within your support network. Celebrate each other's successes and offer comfort and support during challenging times. This approach ensures that the accountability process is positive and uplifting, not burdensome or discouraging.

Maintaining momentum in ministry requires regular self-reflection. Regularly assess your progress against your goals, identify areas needing improvement, and seek guidance from your accountability partners. This self-assessment should be prayerfully done, seeking God's wisdom and guidance in every decision. Don't shy away from your weaknesses; acknowledge them and seek help from others. This vulnerability is a testament to your humility and commitment to growth.

The power of shared accountability extends beyond simply staying on task; it's about fostering spiritual growth and deepening your relationship with God. As you share your experiences and seek advice from others, you'll gain a richer understanding of God's character and His plans for your life. You'll also learn to rely more on

God's strength and wisdom rather than solely on your own resources. This collaborative journey of faith deepens your spiritual maturity and allows you to serve God more effectively.

Building a strong support network and embracing accountability is a continuous process. It requires intentionality, vulnerability, and a commitment to fostering authentic relationships. It's about recognizing your limitations and seeking the help and support of fellow believers. It's a recognition that God often uses others to accomplish His purposes, that we are not meant to walk this journey alone. By embracing accountability and support, you not only maintain momentum but also deepen your faith, strengthen your relationships, and ultimately serve God more effectively. This collaborative approach allows you to leverage the strengths of your support network, maximizing your impact for His glory. Consider this journey a testament to the power of community, a reflection of the body of Christ working together in unity and purpose. This isn't just about achieving individual goals; it's about building a kingdom, together.

Remember, the journey of building a God-honoring ministry is a marathon, not a sprint. There will be times of great progress and times of seemingly little movement. The key is to maintain your focus on God's purpose, persevere through challenges, and celebrate the victories along the way. Surround yourself with a supportive community, embrace accountability, and trust in God's unwavering support. He will equip you for the task, empowering you to overcome obstacles and make a lasting impact for His Kingdom.

Your ministry is not solely your responsibility; it's a collaborative effort fueled by faith, sustained by prayer, and strengthened by the bonds of Christian community. Embrace this truth, and watch your ministry flourish under God's grace. The journey is ongoing, the partnership enduring, and the rewards eternal.

Biblical Examples of Perseverance

The unwavering faith and perseverance demonstrated by biblical figures offer profound lessons for those navigating the challenges of building a God-honoring ministry. Their lives, meticulously documented in Scripture, serve as a powerful testament to the enduring strength found in unwavering commitment to God's purpose, even amidst seemingly insurmountable obstacles.

Examining their experiences, their struggles, and ultimately their triumphs, reveals invaluable strategies we can apply to our own ministries, providing encouragement and practical guidance in our own journeys.

Consider the life of Joseph, a powerful illustration of perseverance in the face of profound adversity. Sold into slavery by his brothers, falsely accused and imprisoned, Joseph endured years of hardship and injustice. Yet, through it all, he maintained his integrity and his faith in God. His unwavering trust, even in the darkest moments, ultimately led to his elevation to a position of immense power in Egypt, where he was able to save his family and countless others from famine. Joseph's story isn't simply a tale of rags to riches; it's a profound demonstration of God's faithfulness, even when circumstances seem hopelessly bleak. His unwavering commitment to righteousness, even when surrounded by temptation and betrayal, serves as a powerful example of perseverance rooted in faith. He didn't allow his circumstances to define him; instead, he allowed his faith to shape his response to adversity. This is a crucial lesson for ministry builders – our faith, not our feelings, must guide our actions, especially during challenging seasons. Joseph's story reminds us that God often uses our trials to refine us, prepare us, and ultimately use us for His greater glory. The seemingly endless cycle of betrayal and hardship did not extinguish Joseph's faith; rather, it strengthened it, shaping him into the instrument God intended him to be. We too can learn from his example, cultivating resilience and unwavering faith to navigate the inevitable challenges on our ministry path.

Another compelling example is found in the life of David, the shepherd boy who became king of Israel. His journey was far from smooth. He faced fierce opposition from Saul, the reigning king, who sought to kill him. He endured exile, betrayal, and numerous battles. Yet, David's unwavering faith in God, coupled with his courage and determination, enabled him to overcome these challenges and ultimately fulfill God's purpose for his life. David's story highlights the importance of trusting God's timing. He didn't force his way to the throne; he patiently waited upon the Lord, even when it seemed like his opportunities were fading. This is a vital lesson for ministry building – rushing ahead of God's plan can often lead to setbacks and discouragement. The waiting period can feel agonizing, filled with doubt and uncertainty, but David's example reminds us that God's timing is perfect. It may not be our timing, but it is always the right timing. His deep devotion and prayerful reliance on God fueled his perseverance, proving the effectiveness of seeking God's guidance and strength throughout every stage of his life and ministry. The seemingly insurmountable obstacles – the relentless pursuit by Saul, the betrayals of those closest to him –never extinguished his faith or his commitment to God's calling.

Rather, they served as opportunities for spiritual growth, strengthening his reliance on God and shaping his character into that of a king known for his faith and devotion. David's life teaches us that perseverance, sustained by unwavering faith and prayer, is a powerful force that can overcome any obstacle.

The apostle Paul's life offers a powerful illustration of unwavering perseverance amidst intense persecution. Imprisoned, beaten, and shipwrecked, he faced relentless opposition to his ministry. Yet, he remained steadfast in his commitment to spreading the Gospel. His letters, brimming with encouragement and unwavering faith, testify to his unwavering dedication, even in the face of immense suffering. Paul's unwavering determination reveals the crucial role of purpose in sustaining perseverance. His clear understanding of God's calling, his conviction about the importance of the Gospel, fueled his endurance and sustained his faith. This deep sense of purpose served as his anchor, helping him navigate stormy seas and withstand fierce opposition. We can learn from Paul's example to clarify our own ministry purpose, ensuring that it aligns with God's calling and strengthens our commitment during challenging times. His relentless pursuit of sharing the Gospel is a compelling example of perseverance in action, inspiring us to remain committed to our own ministry objectives, regardless of the difficulties encountered.

Paul's story is a testament to the power of faith to overcome adversity and a reminder that even amidst seemingly insurmountable obstacles, our commitment to God's purpose can fuel our perseverance. His unwavering belief in God's plan for his life and his commitment to sharing the Gospel, even in the face of death, serve as a profound example for us to emulate.

Furthermore, the prophet Elijah provides a potent example of perseverance amid doubt and despair. After his triumphant victory on Mount Carmel, Elijah fled into the wilderness, overwhelmed by Jezebel's threat. Exhausted and despondent, he pleaded with God to end his life. Yet, God strengthened and sustained him, demonstrating that even the most faithful can experience moments of weakness and doubt. Elijah's experience highlights the critical importance of self-care and seeking support during challenging seasons. Feeling overwhelmed by external pressures and battling internal conflicts, Elijah demonstrates the human side of faith – the vulnerability, the exhaustion, the doubt. But his story doesn't end there. God's intervention, his provision of sustenance and strength, ultimately renewed Elijah's spirit and enabled him to continue his prophetic ministry. This underscores the vital role of relying on God's strength during times of weakness. We too must remember that it's okay to acknowledge our struggles, our doubts, our moments of weakness. It's in these vulnerable moments that we can find God's strength most powerfully. Elijah's story reminds us that seeking refuge in God's presence, admitting our vulnerability, and seeking support are essential components of perseverance. It is through these moments of vulnerability that we can most profoundly experience God's grace and renewed strength, helping us to persevere in our ministry journey.

These biblical examples—Joseph's unwavering faith in the face of injustice, David's steadfast trust in God's timing, Paul's relentless dedication despite persecution, and Elijah's resilience despite discouragement—offer invaluable lessons for building a sustainable and God-honoring ministry. They illustrate the importance of faith, perseverance, prayer, community support, and a clear understanding of God's purpose. Their journeys, marked by both triumph and tribulation, serve as beacons of hope, inspiring us to press on, even when faced with adversity. The stories are not merely historical accounts; they are living testimonies to the power of faith, reminding us that God's grace is sufficient, His strength is made perfect in weakness, and His purpose will ultimately prevail.

Embrace these lessons, learn from these examples, and let their stories empower you on your own journey to building a ministry that glorifies God. Remember that the path is not always easy, but with faith, perseverance, and the unwavering support of God and your community, you can overcome any obstacle and achieve His divine purpose for your life and ministry. The lessons from these biblical figures are timeless and universally applicable; they serve as a constant source of encouragement and inspiration to anyone who seeks to serve God faithfully, irrespective of the challenges they face along the way. The journey may be long and arduous, but the reward of faithfully serving God far surpasses any temporary hardship.

Giving Back and Serving Others

The previous section explored the unwavering faith and perseverance of biblical figures as models for building a God-honoring ministry. Now, let's shift our focus to a crucial element of a purposeful life: giving back and serving others. This isn't merely an add-on to our spiritual journey; it is integral to its very core. Serving others isn't just about acts of charity; it's about actively participating in God's redemptive work in the world, mirroring Christ's selfless love and sacrifice.

The inherent human desire to make a difference transcends cultural and religious boundaries. We are created in God's image, and that image reflects a compassionate, giving nature. When we act in accordance with this inherent goodness, we experience a profound sense of fulfillment, a joy that surpasses any material reward. This joy stems from aligning our actions with God's purpose – a purpose that inherently involves extending love and support to those around us. It's a principle echoed throughout scripture, from the parable of the Good Samaritan to Christ's own ministry, which was characterized by unwavering service and compassion.

Identifying opportunities for service requires introspection and a willingness to look beyond ourselves. Ask yourself: What are my unique gifts and talents? How can I utilize these abilities to address the needs of others? Perhaps you possess strong organizational skills that could benefit a local charity, or exceptional communication skills that could be used to mentor at-risk youth. Maybe you have a knack for crafting or gardening, allowing you to create beautiful items to sell for a cause or cultivate a community garden. The possibilities are as limitless as your creativity and willingness to serve.

Don't underestimate the power of small acts of service. A simple act of kindness, a listening ear, a helping hand – these seemingly minor gestures can have a profound impact on someone's life. Remember the woman who anointed Jesus' feet with expensive perfume? Her seemingly extravagant act of service was deemed worthy of mention in the Gospels, highlighting the significance of even seemingly insignificant gestures offered with love and devotion. Similarly, your acts of service, however small they might seem, are seen and valued by God.

Volunteering is a wonderful avenue for extending your service. Countless organizations rely on volunteers to carry out their essential work. From soup kitchens and homeless shelters to hospitals and animal rescues, there is a vast array of opportunities to contribute your time and skills to a cause you care about. The experience itself is deeply enriching; it allows you to connect with others, learn new skills, and witness firsthand the positive impact your efforts have on those you serve. Beyond the tangible benefits, volunteering cultivates humility, empathy, and a deeper appreciation for the blessings in your own life.

Mentoring offers another fulfilling path to service. Sharing your knowledge, experience, and wisdom with others can be incredibly transformative, both for the mentor and the mentee. Consider mentoring a young person, a fellow church member, or someone in your professional field. Your guidance can help them navigate challenges, achieve their goals, and develop their potential. This act of mentorship is an investment in the Kingdom of God, fostering growth and nurturing future generations of servants.

Beyond formal volunteering and mentoring, countless opportunities for service exist within your daily life. Engage in acts of random kindness – hold a door open for someone, offer to help a neighbor with yard work, or simply offer a kind word to a stranger. These small gestures, often overlooked, radiate God's love and have the power to transform someone's day, if not their entire perspective.

Serving others isn't about seeking recognition or applause; it's about expressing your love for God through acts of love for your fellow human beings. It's about aligning your life with God's purpose, demonstrating His grace and compassion to a world that desperately needs it. When you serve others, you are not simply helping them; you are also helping yourself. You are cultivating a spirit of humility, expanding your empathy, and experiencing the profound joy that comes from living a life of purpose.

The act of serving often reveals hidden talents and strengths you might not have been aware of. The challenges you encounter while serving others will often push you to grow and develop in unexpected ways. You'll learn to problem-solve, adapt, and collaborate with others, all while strengthening your faith and deepening your relationship with God. These experiences, both big and small, contribute to your personal growth and spiritual development, shaping you into the person God created you to be.

Remember the parable of the talents in Matthew 25:14-30. The master entrusted his servants with different amounts of talents, expecting them to use their gifts wisely. Similarly, God has given each of us unique talents and abilities, expecting us to employ them in service to Him and others. The story underscores the importance of not burying our talents but utilizing them to their full potential for the greater good.

The benefits of serving extend beyond the individual; they ripple outwards to affect communities and society as a whole. When we actively participate in serving others, we build stronger communities, fostering a sense of belonging and mutual support. We address societal needs, contributing to a more just and equitable world. Our actions serve as a testament to the transformative power of faith and inspire others to follow suit.

Serving others shouldn't feel like a burden or an obligation, but rather a privilege and a joy. When approached with the right attitude, serving others becomes a deeply fulfilling experience, strengthening our relationship with God and enriching our lives in countless ways. It allows us to step outside our own concerns and focus on the needs of others, fostering empathy and compassion.

This selfless act often leads to unexpected blessings and opportunities for personal growth. The rewards of serving may not always be immediate or apparent, but they are immeasurable in the long run.

This journey of service is a lifelong commitment, a continuous process of growth and discovery. It's about consistently seeking opportunities to use your gifts and talents for the benefit of others, reflecting the love of Christ in your actions. It's not about perfection, but about a willingness to serve with a humble heart and a compassionate spirit. Even seemingly small acts of kindness can have a significant impact, radiating God's love and making the world a more compassionate place. Embrace this journey of service, and let it transform your life and the lives of those around you. Remember, true fulfillment lies not in accumulating possessions or achieving worldly success, but in living a life of purpose, marked by selfless service and unwavering faith. As you embark on this journey of giving back and serving others, trust in God's guidance, rely on His strength, and let His love be your guiding light. The rewards are far greater than you can imagine.

Maintaining a Spirit of Gratitude

The previous section emphasized the vital role of selfless service in living a purposeful Christian life, mirroring Christ's example of unwavering love and sacrifice. Now, we transition to another cornerstone of a fulfilling and God-centered existence: cultivating a spirit of gratitude. This isn't merely about politeness or good manners; it's a fundamental spiritual discipline that profoundly impacts our perspective, our relationships, and our ability to discern God's purpose for our lives. A grateful heart is a receptive heart, open to receiving the blessings God continuously pours out upon us, both big and small.

Gratitude isn't a passive emotion; it's an active choice. It's a conscious decision to focus on the positive aspects of our lives, acknowledging the goodness of God even amidst challenges and difficulties. This isn't about ignoring hardship or pretending problems don't exist; rather, it's about choosing to see God's hand at work even in the midst of storms. It's about recognizing His provision, His protection, and His unwavering love, even when we don't fully understand His plan.

Consider the countless ways God blesses us daily. We often take these blessings for granted – the air we breathe, the food we eat, the shelter over our heads, the health we enjoy (or the healing we experience), the love of family and friends, the opportunities that present themselves. These are all manifestations of God's grace, His boundless love poured out upon us. When we cultivate a spirit of gratitude, we begin to see these blessings with fresh eyes, appreciating their value and acknowledging their source.

One of the most effective ways to cultivate gratitude is through consistent practice. Make it a habit to consciously acknowledge and express your thankfulness throughout the day. This could be a simple prayer before meals, a moment of reflection before bed, or a written journal entry where you list specific things you're thankful for. Even a few moments of mindful appreciation can significantly shift your perspective and create a more positive emotional state.

Journaling is a powerful tool for cultivating gratitude. The act of writing down your blessings forces you to slow down, reflect, and appreciate the details of your life. Don't just list generic items like "family" or "health"; be specific. Did your child say something particularly sweet today? Did a friend offer unexpected support? Did you witness a beautiful sunset? Record these specific moments of gratitude, noting the emotions they evoked and how they connected you to God's goodness. Over time, reviewing your gratitude journal can be a source of encouragement, reminding you of God's faithfulness throughout your life's journey.

Prayer is another powerful vehicle for expressing gratitude. Don't limit your prayers to requests or petitions; make a conscious effort to thank God for His blessings. Share your heartfelt appreciation for the specific ways He's touched your life, both big and small. This act of worship not only deepens your relationship with God but also fosters a spirit of humility and dependence upon Him. Remember, gratitude is not simply a religious exercise; it's a fundamental act of faith, acknowledging God's sovereignty and His constant presence in our lives.

Beyond personal journaling and prayer, express your gratitude to others. A simple "thank you" can have a profound impact on someone's day. Take the time to acknowledge the kindnesses and efforts of those around you, expressing your sincere appreciation for their contributions to your life. This not only strengthens relationships but also models a grateful heart for others to emulate. Consider sending thank-you notes, expressing your appreciation for a gift, a helping hand, or a kind word. In our busy lives, a thoughtful gesture of gratitude can go a long way in building stronger bonds and spreading positivity.

It's important to note that cultivating gratitude isn't about ignoring the negative aspects of life. We all face challenges, setbacks, and disappointments. However, gratitude allows us to approach these difficulties with a different perspective. Instead of dwelling on what we lack or what's gone wrong, we can focus on what we have and what remains in our lives. This isn't about toxic positivity, where we deny pain or hardship; rather, it's about finding the silver linings, the unexpected blessings that often emerge even from difficult circumstances. In the midst of hardship, gratitude allows us to remain rooted in faith, trusting in God's plan even when it's difficult to understand.

For example, perhaps you've faced a significant financial setback. Instead of focusing solely on the loss, reflect on the ways God has provided for you in the past, the support you've received from family and friends, and the opportunities for growth that may arise from this difficult experience. Perhaps a job loss has led to the discovery of a new career path that is even more fulfilling, or a health crisis has caused a renewed appreciation for the gift of life and the importance of nurturing relationships. These "silver linings" are often difficult to see amidst the storm, but with a grateful heart, we're more likely to recognize them and find hope in the midst of adversity.

Furthermore, cultivating a spirit of gratitude has profound implications for our physical and mental well-being. Numerous studies have shown a strong correlation between gratitude and increased happiness, reduced stress, improved sleep, and a stronger immune system. This is because gratitude shifts our focus from what we lack to what we have, fostering a more positive outlook and reducing the impact of negativity. When we're grateful, we're less likely to dwell on anxieties or worries, allowing us to approach challenges with greater resilience and peace.

To actively cultivate a spirit of gratitude, consider incorporating these practices into your daily routine:

Start and end your day with gratitude: Before you even get out of bed, take a few moments to reflect on what you're thankful for. Similarly, before bed, review the day, focusing on the positive experiences and expressing your thanks to God for his blessings.

Keep a gratitude journal: This doesn't have to be elaborate; a simple notebook or even a digital document will suffice. Regularly write down specific things you're grateful for, including details and emotions associated with these experiences. Go check out DivineWarriorLifeCoaching. com, AlishaJacksonMinistries.org, ABetterLifePublishingCompany. com, FaithConnectionCenter.org, AlishaJacksonAcademy.com and www.HealingWithinTransformationCenter.com for additional transformational tools, such as the gratitude and speak life journals.

Express gratitude to others: Take time to verbally thank people for their kindnesses and support. Send handwritten thank-you notes or emails expressing your appreciation. These acts of gratitude not only strengthen relationships but also boost your own emotional well-being.

Practice mindful appreciation: Pause throughout the day to appreciate the small things – the warmth of the sun, the beauty of nature, a delicious meal, or a kind gesture from a stranger. These small moments of appreciation can have a profound impact on your overall sense of well-being.

Practice forgiveness: Holding onto bitterness and resentment prevents us from experiencing gratitude. Forgiveness is a crucial component of a grateful heart, allowing us to let go of negativity and focus on the positive aspects of our lives.

Living a life of purpose isn't solely about achieving great things or accomplishing ambitious goals. It's also about cultivating a deep and abiding sense of gratitude for God's love, His provision, and His unwavering presence in our lives. By consistently practicing gratitude, we open our hearts to receive His blessings, we strengthen our faith, and we experience a profound sense of peace and joy that transcends the challenges and uncertainties of life. Remember, gratitude is not a one-time event, but a lifelong journey– a continuous process of recognizing and appreciating God's immeasurable grace and His endless love. Embrace this journey, and watch as it transforms your life from the inside out. The rewards are far greater than you can imagine – a heart overflowing with joy, a spirit filled with peace, and a life lived in profound gratitude for the blessings God has bestowed upon you.

Trusting Gods Guidance and Timing

Having cultivated a heart overflowing with gratitude, we now embark on another crucial aspect of living a purposeful Christian life: trusting in God's guidance and timing. This isn't about passive resignation; it's about active faith—a confident belief that God's plan for your life is perfect, even if the path seems unclear or the timing perplexing. This trust, nurtured through consistent prayer, meditation, and seeking spiritual counsel, becomes the bedrock upon which a life of purpose is built. It's a journey of faith, not a destination of instant gratification.

Uncertainty is an inherent part of the human experience. We crave predictability, security, and control. Yet, life often throws curveballs—unexpected challenges, unforeseen opportunities, and detours that seem to lead us away from our perceived goals. In these moments, clinging to God's promises and trusting in His perfect timing becomes paramount. It requires a conscious decision to relinquish our need for control and to surrender our anxieties to the One who holds the future in His hands. This isn't about blindly following a predetermined path, but rather about actively seeking God's direction and then trusting His lead with unwavering faith.

How, then, do we cultivate this unwavering trust? It begins with a deep understanding of God's character. He is not a distant, uncaring deity, but a loving Father who intimately knows our hearts and desires. He sees the bigger picture, the panoramic view of our lives that we, with our limited perspectives, often miss. His timing is never arbitrary; it's always orchestrated with divine purpose and wisdom. Isaiah 55:8-9 beautifully captures this truth: "For my thoughts are not your thoughts, neither are your ways my ways, "declares the Lord. "As the heavens are higher than the earth, so are my ways higher than your ways and my thoughts than your thoughts."

Prayer is the lifeline that connects us to God's guidance. It's not merely a ritualistic recitation of words, but a heartfelt conversation with our Heavenly Father. Through prayer, we pour out our anxieties, seek His wisdom, and invite His presence into our lives.

This involves honest and vulnerable communication, sharing both our joys and our struggles. It's about actively listening for His still, small voice, a gentle whisper that guides us towards His intended path. Consider keeping a prayer journal – recording your prayers and noting any insights or promptings you receive. This record can become a powerful testament to God's faithfulness and guidance over time.

Meditation, another vital spiritual discipline, allows us to quiet our minds and focus on God's presence. It's a time of stillness and reflection, where we can clear away the mental clutter and connect with the divine. In this quiet space, we become more receptive to His guidance, allowing His wisdom to permeate our thoughts and actions. This may involve spending time in nature, listening to calming music, or simply focusing on a scripture verse. The key is to create a peaceful environment where you can connect with God on a deeper level. Regular meditation cultivates inner peace and strengthens your ability to discern God's will for your life.

Seeking spiritual guidance from trusted mentors, pastors, or spiritual advisors can also significantly enhance our ability to trust God's timing. These individuals, experienced in navigating life's challenges and discerning God's will, can offer invaluable insights and support. They can help us to clarify our thoughts, identify potential blind spots, and discern God's voice amidst the noise of the world. Remember, seeking counsel is not a sign of weakness but a sign of wisdom and a recognition of the importance of community in our spiritual journey. Choose advisors who are grounded in scripture, experienced in spiritual discernment, and possess wisdom that can help navigate your path.

Trusting God's timing doesn't mean passively waiting for things to happen. It means actively pursuing the opportunities that He presents, while simultaneously surrendering our anxieties about the timing. It's a dance between proactive engagement and peaceful surrender. This might involve taking a leap of faith, pursuing a new career path, or stepping out of your comfort zone to serve others. The key is to discern whether these steps are aligned with God's guidance, which often involves seeking prayerful counsel and listening for His prompting.

Consider the parable of the talents in Matthew 25:14-30. The master entrusted his servants with different talents, and those who diligently used their talents, regardless of the amount, were commended. Similarly, God entrusts each of us with unique gifts and abilities. Our task is to utilize these gifts for His glory, trusting that He will provide the opportunities and resources needed at the right time. We may not understand the "why" behind the timing, but we can trust in His perfect plan.

Furthermore, consider the story of Joseph in the Book of Genesis. His life was filled with unexpected twists and turns—betrayal by his brothers, wrongful imprisonment, and periods of uncertainty. Yet, through it all, he maintained his faith in God, trusting that His plans were greater than his circumstances. Ultimately, Joseph's unwavering faith led him to a position of power and influence, where he was able to save his family and his nation from famine. His story is a powerful testament to the fact that God's timing, even when seemingly delayed or difficult, ultimately leads to His perfect purpose.

Delayed opportunities are often opportunities disguised. God may be using the time of waiting to prepare you for something greater, shaping your character, refining your skills, or strengthening your faith. This waiting period, while sometimes challenging, provides time for growth, reflection, and deepening reliance on God's guidance. Embrace these moments not as setbacks, but as seasons of preparation and refinement. Use this time to develop your spiritual disciplines, strengthen your relationships, and prepare yourself for the tasks God has in store.

The journey of trusting in God's timing and guidance is a lifelong process, not a one-time event. It involves consistent prayer, meditation, seeking spiritual guidance, and actively pursuing opportunities that align with God's will. Remember that moments of doubt and uncertainty are inevitable, but these moments should strengthen our reliance on His promises. The peace that transcends understanding is a reward for trusting His perfect timing, allowing serenity to bloom in the midst of life's complexities. This trust will not only guide you toward fulfilling your God-given purpose but will also bring a profound sense of peace and joy that surpasses all understanding. Remember, God's timing is always perfect, even when it doesn't feel that way. Embrace the journey, trusting that He is leading you every step of the way. And as you do, you will experience the transformative power of a life lived in unwavering faith and confident trust in your loving Father.

Continuing to Learn and Grow

The journey of faith, as we've explored, is not a static state but a dynamic, ever-evolving process. Just as a seed requires nurturing to blossom into a mighty tree, so too does our spiritual life demand continuous cultivation. This nurturing takes the form of ongoing learning and personal growth, a commitment that extends far beyond the initial acceptance of faith. It's a lifelong pursuit that intertwines our spiritual development with our professional and personal aspirations, creating a harmonious tapestry of purpose-driven living.

This commitment to lifelong learning isn't merely about accumulating knowledge; it's about fostering a growth mindset—a belief that our abilities are not fixed but can be developed through dedication and perseverance. This mindset is crucial for navigating the ever-changing landscapes of life and ministry. The world is constantly evolving, presenting new challenges and opportunities. To remain effective and impactful in our chosen fields, we must adapt and grow alongside it. This adaptability isn't just beneficial for professional success; it's vital for effectively serving God and others.

Consider the parable of the talents in Matthew 25. The servants who doubled their master's investments weren't praised for their initial abilities but for their willingness to use their talents wisely and productively. They actively sought opportunities to grow their skills and contribute meaningfully. Their success wasn't solely based on innate talent; it was a testament to their proactive approach to growth and development. This proactive approach, this consistent commitment to self-improvement, is the very essence of lifelong learning.

How then do we practically incorporate this commitment into our daily lives? The avenues are diverse and plentiful. Firstly, engaging in continuous education is paramount. This doesn't necessarily mean returning to formal schooling, though it certainly could. It encompasses a much broader spectrum of learning experiences.

Think of online courses, workshops, seminars, conferences, and even engaging with insightful books and articles related to your profession, spiritual growth, or personal interests. The beauty of the digital age is its accessibility to a wealth of knowledge. Countless platforms offer online courses on practically any subject imaginable, allowing us to learn at our own pace and convenience. These platforms cater to diverse learning styles, incorporating video lectures, interactive exercises, and community forums, creating a dynamic and engaging learning environment. Moreover, many reputable organizations offer free or low-cost courses, making continuous education accessible to individuals regardless of their financial situation, such as AlishaJacksonAcademy.com.

Beyond formal learning, there's immense value in seeking out mentors and engaging in peer learning. A mentor can provide invaluable guidance, support, and encouragement, offering a seasoned perspective on navigating professional and spiritual challenges. Mentorship isn't just about receiving advice; it's about building a relationship, learning from someone's experiences, and gaining a deeper understanding of oneself. Similarly, peer learning, engaging with others who share similar goals and aspirations, creates a supportive environment for mutual growth and encouragement. Through collaborative learning, we learn from each other's strengths and experiences, expanding our perspectives and enhancing our learning journey.

Further, personal development activities play a crucial role in continuous growth. This involves practices such as journaling, mindfulness meditation, prayer, and engaging in activities that foster self-awareness and emotional intelligence. Journaling allows us to reflect on our experiences, identify patterns, and gain a deeper understanding of ourselves. Mindfulness meditation, on the other hand, cultivates present moment awareness, reducing stress and enhancing focus. Prayer, as a form of communication with God, provides guidance, comfort, and strength for navigating life's complexities. Together, these practices contribute to holistic growth, fostering both spiritual maturity and emotional well-being.

Skill development is another crucial aspect of lifelong learning. This involves identifying areas where we can enhance our abilities and proactively seeking opportunities for improvement. This could involve acquiring new skills altogether, such as learning a new language or software program, or honing existing skills to a higher level of proficiency. Skill development is not merely about career advancement; it's about enhancing our capacity to serve others more effectively. The more skilled we become, the more effectively we can contribute to our communities, churches, and the world at large.

The benefits of continuous learning and growth are manifold. Firstly, it enhances our adaptability, equipping us to navigate the ever-changing demands of life and ministry. In today's rapidly evolving world, the ability to adapt is paramount. Continuous learning provides the tools and knowledge necessary to embrace change and thrive amidst uncertainty. Furthermore, it enhances our capacity to serve, allowing us to contribute more meaningfully to our communities and the world. By continually expanding our skills and knowledge, we enhance our ability to meet the needs of others effectively.

Moreover, continuous growth unlocks new opportunities, both professionally and personally. As we develop our skills and expand our knowledge, we open ourselves to a wider range of possibilities. These opportunities may lead to career advancements, new relationships, or simply a deeper sense of fulfillment and purpose. These opportunities are not merely a matter of chance; they are the result of our proactive commitment to growth and development.

Finally, and perhaps most importantly, continuous learning fosters a deeper relationship with God. As we seek to grow in wisdom, understanding, and grace, we become more attuned to the promptings of the Holy Spirit. We learn to discern God's will more clearly and to align our lives more closely with His purposes. This deeper connection with God is not merely a byproduct of lifelong learning; it is its very foundation. It's a symbiotic relationship, where our pursuit of knowledge and growth deepens our faith and our faith inspires us to learn more. The journey of faith is a lifelong adventure, and continuous learning is the compass that guides us along the way. Embrace this journey; embrace the transformative power of continuous learning, and watch as your life blossoms into its full potential, reflecting the glory of God.

The pursuit of lifelong learning is not a burden but a privilege, a pathway to a richer, more fulfilling life, lived in accordance with God's will and purpose for your life. It is a journey of continuous discovery, both of yourself and of the divine plan unfolding before you. Embrace the challenge, embrace the growth, and experience the joy of a life lived to its fullest potential, guided by the unwavering love and grace of our Heavenly Father. This continuous pursuit will enrich not only your personal life, but will enable you to impact the lives of others in profound and meaningful ways, reflecting the love and grace of Christ to the world. Remember, the journey is as important as the destination; each step you take in pursuit of growth brings you closer to the fulfillment of God's unique plan for your life.

Biblical Examples of
a Life of Purpose

The pursuit of a life of purpose, deeply rooted in faith, finds rich resonance throughout the scriptures. Examining the lives of biblical figures provides invaluable insight and inspiration for our own journeys. These individuals, diverse in their backgrounds and callings, offer a tapestry of examples demonstrating how faith can be interwoven into the fabric of daily life, resulting in a life of profound impact. Their stories are not mere historical accounts; they are living testaments to the transformative power of aligning our lives with God's will.

Consider the life of Joseph, sold into slavery by his brothers, yet rising to become second in command in Egypt. His unwavering faith, even amidst unimaginable hardship, allowed him to interpret dreams and ultimately save his family from famine. Joseph's life wasn't defined by the adversity he faced, but by his persistent faith and his willingness to trust in God's plan, even when it remained unclear. He didn't shy away from his responsibilities, but embraced them with unwavering devotion, even when those responsibilities were seemingly insurmountable. His story teaches us that the path to purpose often winds through unexpected trials, but it is in these trials that our faith is strengthened and our character refined. Joseph's resilience and perseverance, fueled by his steadfast faith, serve as a powerful reminder that even in the darkest of times, God's hand is at work, guiding us towards our ultimate purpose. His story is not just about individual perseverance, but also about the ripple effect of a life lived in obedience to God; his actions saved countless lives and profoundly impacted the trajectory of his family and nation.

The unwavering faith of Esther, a Jewish woman who became queen of Persia, similarly highlights the potential for divine purpose to manifest in unexpected places. Faced with the threat of genocide against her people, Esther bravely risked her own life to approach the king, pleading for the safety of her people. Her courageous act, borne out of deep faith and a profound sense of responsibility, averted a catastrophic tragedy. Esther's story underscores the importance of recognizing and embracing our unique callings, even when those callings may seem daunting or even life-threatening. She didn't seek out this responsibility; it found her in the midst of her ordinary life. This emphasizes that God's plan often unfolds in unexpected ways, calling us to act with courage and faith even when we feel ill-equipped or unprepared. Her obedience to God, coupled with her courageous action, serves as a profound example of how faith can lead to remarkable and even life-saving outcomes. The ripple effect of Esther's faith extended far beyond her personal circumstances, preserving a nation and reminding us of the power of a single individual, acting in accordance with God's will, to impact the course of history.

David, the shepherd boy who became king of Israel, provides another compelling example. His life, marked by both triumph and adversity, demonstrates the importance of humility and reliance on God. From facing Goliath with unwavering faith to navigating the complexities of kingship, David's journey reveals the ongoing process of seeking God's guidance and surrendering to His will.

David's life, filled with both moments of profound success and devastating failures, underscores the importance of acknowledging both our triumphs and our shortcomings. His journey is not one of seamless perfection, but rather a testament to the enduring grace and forgiveness of God. David's consistent return to God amidst his mistakes emphasizes the ongoing nature of faith and the continuous need for repentance and reconciliation. His psalms, imbued with raw emotion and heartfelt vulnerability, offer a glimpse into the inner struggles of a man striving to live a life pleasing to God, demonstrating that a life of purpose isn't about flawless execution, but about persistent devotion and repentance.

The apostle Paul's life, a dramatic transformation from persecutor of Christians to one of Christianity's most influential figures, offers a powerful illustration of the transformative power of faith. His journey exemplifies the radical shift that can occur when we encounter God's love and embrace His purpose for our lives. Paul's unwavering dedication to spreading the Gospel, despite facing immense persecution and hardship, stands as a testament to the enduring power of faith to overcome even the most formidable obstacles. His tireless missionary journeys, fraught with danger and difficulty, serve as a powerful example of unwavering commitment to God's plan. Paul's writings, which form a significant portion of the New Testament, continue to inspire and guide believers centuries later, demonstrating the lasting impact of a life lived in selfless devotion to God's will. His life is a testament to the transforming power of God's grace and the enduring legacy of a life lived in service to others. His unwavering faith in the face of immense adversity serves as an inspiration for us all.

These are but a few of the many biblical examples of individuals who lived lives of purpose, deeply intertwined with their faith. Their stories, filled with challenges, triumphs, and unwavering faith, offer a profound source of inspiration and guidance. They demonstrate that a life of purpose is not a destination but a journey, one that requires continuous growth, perseverance, and an unwavering commitment to God's will. These individuals, while vastly different in their backgrounds and circumstances, share a common thread: a deep and abiding faith that guided their actions and shaped their destinies. Their lives serve as a beacon, illuminating the path towards a life of meaning and purpose, a life lived in accordance with God's plan.

The overarching lesson from these biblical examples is the importance of actively seeking God's will for our lives. It's not a passive pursuit; it requires prayer, reflection, and a willingness to listen to the subtle whispers of the Holy Spirit. It involves identifying our gifts and talents, and discerning how we can utilize these gifts to serve God and others. It's about aligning our ambitions with God's purpose, allowing Him to shape our path and guide our steps. It's about understanding that our purpose is not solely defined by our achievements or accomplishments, but by our commitment to living a life that reflects God's love and grace.

Furthermore, the examples show that a life of purpose is not without hardship. Joseph, Esther, David, and Paul all faced significant challenges and adversity. Yet, it was their unwavering faith that sustained them, enabling them to persevere and ultimately fulfill God's purpose for their lives. This underscores the importance of resilience, the ability to bounce back from setbacks and continue striving towards our goals, even when faced with seemingly insurmountable obstacles. The journey is rarely smooth; it's often marked by unexpected twists and turns, periods of doubt and uncertainty, and moments of intense struggle. However, it's in these challenges that our faith is tested and refined, and our character strengthened.

The biblical examples also highlight the interconnectedness of our lives with the lives of others. Joseph's actions saved his family from famine; Esther's courage saved her people from genocide; David's leadership guided his nation; and Paul's ministry transformed countless lives. This emphasizes that our purpose extends beyond our personal ambitions; it encompasses our relationships with others and our impact on the world around us. Our lives are not lived in isolation; we are interconnected members of God's family, called to love and serve one another. Living a life of purpose, therefore, involves recognizing and embracing our responsibility to contribute to the well-being of others. It's about extending compassion, empathy, and kindness, and using our gifts and talents to make a positive difference in the lives of those around us.

Final Conclusion

You are living proof that being overlooked does not mean being forgotten. In God's Kingdom, the last shall become first, and the forgotten are the ones He raises to display His glory. Through this journey, you have learned that your value was never determined by man's opinion but by God's eternal love and divine purpose for you. Now that you have faced so much-the battles, the heartbreaks, the seasons of waiting-God is now turning the overlooked into the overflowed with blessings. Be in expectation. Stay ready. Continue doing the good works He has placed in your hands, knowing that your labor has never been in vain. The seeds of faith, perseverance, gratitude, prayer, and bold identity you have sown are about to yield a harvest beyond anything you could ever imagine. Your overflow will not only bless you, but it will pour out onto everyone connected to your destiny.

Considering all you have learned, you should now better understand that the biblical examples of purposeful living provide a rich and inspiring framework for your own life. They demonstrate the transformative power of faith, the importance of resilience, and the interconnectedness of out lives with others. By studying these examples and applying what you've learned, you gain valuable insights and guidance as you embark on your own journey of faith and purpose.

Let us draw inspiration from these powerful stories and strive to live lives that reflect God's love, grace, and unwavering purpose. May you, too, leave a lasting legacy of faith, compassion, and service-impacting the lives of others and fulfilling the unique purpose God as ordained for you.

This journey, though challenging at times, is ultimately one of immense reward-the joy of knowing your life is aligned with God's will and that you are making a tangible difference in the world. **Embrace the challenge. Step boldly into your overflow. Walk this path with courage, faith, and unwavering determination.**

"No eye has seen, no ear has heard, and no mind has imagined what God has prepared for those who love him." (**1 Corinthians 2:9, NLT**)

Get ready-your overflow is here. Receive it with open hands, a surrendered heart, and unstoppable faith.

Acknowledgments

This book would not have been possible without the unwavering support and encouragement of many individuals. My deepest gratitude goes to my family, whose love and patience sustained me throughout the writing process. I am especially thankful to Jasmyn, Ariah, Augustine whose love, encouragement, and support is invaluable. I also wish to express my sincere appreciation to my editor, Charlyn Samson, for their insightful guidance and meticulous attention to detail. Their expertise helped shape this book into its final form. Finally, I thank all those who shared their personal stories and experiences, inspiring the reflections and insights within these pages. Their willingness to be vulnerable and open has enriched this work immeasurably. To God be the glory for the strength and guidance provided throughout this endeavor.

Final Prayer

Father God,

Thank You for seeing me when the world overlooked me. Thank You for calling me chosen, beloved, and royal. I surrender my life into Your hands. I receive the overflow You have prepared for me-spiritually, mentally, emotionally, financially, relationally, and physically. Give me the strength to walk boldly in my divine identity. Help me to steward the blessings with wisdom, humility, and faithfulness. May my life be a reflection of Your glory and a testimony of Your goodness. I trust Your timing, Your ways, and Your promises. I declare that my season of overflow is here, and I will walk into it with expectation, obedience, and joy.

In Jesus' mighty name, Amen.

Affirmations

- I am chosen, seen, and loved by God.
- I am walking in my divine purpose and royal identity.
- I am in my season of overflow and blessings.
- I expect good things because God is faithful to His promises.
- I am equipped to steward every blessing with excellence.
- I walk by faith and not by sight.
- I am a living testimony of God's goodness, grace, and power.
- I am deeply rooted in God's love and favor.
- I am a vessel of God's blessings, miracles, and overflow.
- I wise above every obstacle because God's hand is upon me.
- I am an atmosphere-shifter and a blessing-carrier wherever I go.
- I am walking through open doors that no man can shut.
- I am aligned with God's divine timing and perfect plan for my life.
- I radiate confidence, strength, and purpose through Christ.
- I am fruitful in every area of my life because I stay connected to the True Vine.
- I am anointed to prosper, to build, to lead, and to impact.
- I live every day in joyful expectation of God's promises being fulfilled.

Declaration

Today, I boldly declare:

I am no longer overlooked-I am overflowing!

I am stepping into the abundant life God designed for me.

Every promise, every blessing, and every open door that is ordained for me will find me.

I move forward with courage, unwavering faith, and joyful expectation.

I am a royal heir of the Kingdom, and my overflow is unstoppable.

In Jesus' name, it is so, and it shall not be otherwise!

Appendix: Additional Resources for Continued Growth

This appendix provides additional resources for deeper study, reflection, and continued growth on your journey from "Overlooked to Overflow." These tools are designed to strengthen your faith, help you stay rooted in God's promises, and support your spiritual and personal development.

These resources offer opportunities for deeper engagement with the concepts presented and provide avenues for continued spiritual growth and personal development. May they serve as a springboard for your continued journey of faith and purpose.

Recommended Bible Translations:

- **New International Version (NIV)** -
  Clear and contemporary language for easy understanding.
- **New King James Version (NKJV)** -
  Faithful to original texts with modern readability.
- **Amplified Bible (AMP)** -
  Expands meanings of Scriptures for deeper understanding.

Bible Study Tools:

- **YouVersion Bible App** (free app for daily Bible reading, devotionals, and study plans)
  Website: www.bible.com
- **Bible Gateway** (online Bible search and study resource)
  Website: www.biblegateway.com

Recommended Books for Deeper Growth by Alisha Jackson:

- "*I AM A Divine Warrior*"
- "*The Ultimate Emotional Healing eGuide: 50 Healing Scriptures, Affirmations, Reflection Exercises, Journaling Prompts, Prayers, Healing Action Steps for Restoration and a 30-Day Faith Challenge*"
- "*The Forgiveness Prayer Guide: Transform Your Life with Healing Scriptures and Prayer*"

Websites for Christian Growth by Alisha Jackson:

- Alisha Jackson Ministries-
  www.AlishaJacksonMinistries.org
- Faith Connection Center-
  www.FaithConnectionCenter.org
- A Better Life Publishing Company-
  www.ABetterLifePublishingCompany.com
- Divine Warrior Life Coaching-
  www.DivineWarriorLifeCoaching.com
- Alisha Jackson Academy-
  www.AlishaJacksonAcademy.com
- Healing Within Transformation Center-
  www.HealingWithinTransformationCenter.com

Journaling and Gratitude Resources: Christian Gratitude and Speak Life Journal (available on AlishaJacksonAcademy.com and DivineWarriorLifeCoaching.com).

May these resources bless you, strengthen you, and empower you to walk boldly in your divine purpose and overflow.

Bonus Reflection Questions

Tis section will help you to pause, reflect, and apply everything you have learned from *Overlooked to Overflow*. Take a moment to reflect, journal, and pray through these questions as you move forward from being overlooked to living in the overflow of God's blessings. Let the Holy Spirit guide you into deeper revelation and purpose.

Personal Reflection:

1. In what ways have I seen God's faithfulness during seasons of being overlooked?
2. What blessings am I expecting God to overflow into my life in this next season?
3. How has my understanding of my divine identity changes after reading this book?
4. What are the key mindsets I need to continue strengthening to walk fully in my calling?
5. What good works has God prepared in advance for me to walk in (Ephesians 2:10)?
6. How can I remain in a position of gratitude and expectancy daily?
7. What does living as royalty in God's kingdom look like practically in my everyday life?
8. How can I intentionally serve others while living in my overflow?
9. What spiritual disciplines (prayer, journaling, fasting, Bible study) do I need to prioritize more?

10. How will I celebrate and steward the blessings that God is about to release into my life?

Final Encouragement:

Remember: the season of being overlooked was never a rejection-it was God's redirection into divine positioning. Now, walk boldly in the overflow! Stay rooted in gratitude, anchored in prayer, and overflowing with faith. Your best days are not behind you; they are unfolding right now.

Prayer Journal Template

Prayer Journal: My Overflow Season

Today Date: _____

Scripture of the Day:

(Example: *"The Lord will open the heavens, the storehouse of His bounty, to send rain on your land in season and to bless all the work of your hands."* -Deuteronomy 28:12 NIV)

Gratitude List (3 things I'm thankful for today):

1. _____

2. _____

3. _____

Prayer Focus:

(What am I believing God for today!)

_____

_____

_____

Overflow Declarations:

(Write your own faith declaration for your overflow season.) Example: _"Today I walk in divine favor and receive every blessing God has stored up for me."_

_____

_____

_____

Hearing from God:

(Any thoughts, dreams, visions, impressions during prayer time?)

_____

_____

_____

Action Step in Faith:

(What is one thing I will do today to walk in the overflow?)

_____

_____

_____

Reference List

New Life Version. (2003). *Holy Bible: New Life Version.* Barbour Publishing. (Original work published n.d.)

- Acts 9:36–42
- Deuteronomy 28:12
- Ephesians 2:10
- Jeremiah 29:11
- Matthew 13:1–23
- Matthew 25
- Matthew 25:14–30
- Proverbs 31
- 2 Corinthians 12:9
- 1 Chronicles 29
- Proverbs 17:22

Glossary List

Glossary: *Overlooked to Overflow*

This glossary provides definitions of key terms used throughout the book to ensure clarity and understanding.

Accountability – The willingness to accept responsibility for one's actions and growth, especially in one's spiritual walk.

Act of Service – A selfless deed performed to bless or assist others, often viewed as a practical expression of love and faith.

Affirmations – Positive, truth-filled statements used to reinforce identity, purpose, and faith in alignment with God's Word.

Bitterness – A hardened emotional state often stemming from unresolved hurt or unforgiveness, which can hinder spiritual growth.

Commitment – A dedicated choice to remain faithful to God's calling and purpose, even through challenges.

Criticism – Feedback, whether constructive or harmful, that tests personal resilience and humility.

Declarations – Bold, faith-driven statements spoken with confidence, affirming God's promises and one's identity in Him.

Discernment – Spiritual insight and wisdom that helps distinguish truth from deception and guides decision-making aligned with God's will.

Faith – Trust and reliance on God's grace and power, leading to a life of obedience and devotion.

Faith in Action – Living out belief through deeds, decisions, and trust, even when the outcome is unseen.

Forgiveness – The intentional release of resentment, freeing both self and others from emotional bondage.

Goals – Spirit-led objectives that reflect personal growth and alignment with God's vision for one's life.

Gratitude – A heart posture of thankfulness, acknowledging God's blessings in all circumstances.

Growth – The process of spiritual, emotional, and personal development through learning, trials, and obedience.

Immeasurable Worth – The priceless value placed on each person by God, rooted in His love and creation.

Journaling – A reflective practice that captures prayers, insights, emotions, and spiritual revelations.

Journey – The unfolding path of personal and spiritual development marked by seasons of struggle and breakthrough.

Legacy – The enduring impact of a life lived purposefully, influencing future generations.

Motivation – The inner drive fueled by purpose, calling, and a desire to glorify God through one's actions.

Obedience – A deliberate response to God's direction, often requiring trust, humility, and surrender.

Obstacles – Life's challenges that test faith, resilience, and perseverance, often used by God for refinement.

Overflow – A life so filled with God's love, grace, and purpose that it abundantly blesses others.

Overlooked – A feeling or reality of being unseen or underestimated, often a setup for divine elevation.

Perseverance – Continued effort and faith despite trials or setbacks, anchored in hope and trust in God.

Positive – A hopeful, faith-filled perspective that seeks God's goodness in every circumstance.

Prayer – A sacred conversation with God, offering praise, seeking guidance, and deepening relationship.

Proactive Approach – Taking intentional steps toward healing, purpose, and obedience rather than waiting passively.

Purpose – A divinely ordained reason for existence, often involving service to others and the fulfillment of God's will.

Refinement – The process by which God purifies and shapes a person's character through challenges and growth.

Reflection – Intentional time to ponder one's life, choices, and God's guidance, often leading to clarity and transformation.

Rejection – An experience of being turned away or excluded, often used by God to redirect and strengthen identity.

Resilience – The ability to recover from adversity, maintaining a strong spiritual foundation amidst challenges.

Self-Acceptance – Embracing oneself as God created, including strengths and flaws, through the lens of grace.

Self-Aggrandizement – The act of excessively promoting oneself, which can hinder humility and spiritual maturity.

Self-Care – Nourishing the mind, body, and spirit with rest, boundaries, and practices that honor God and self.

Self-Development – The ongoing process of becoming the best version of oneself through learning and God's guidance.

Self-Discovery – The unfolding understanding of one's identity, values, and purpose, led by the Holy Spirit.

Self-Doubt – Uncertainty about one's abilities or worth, often countered through faith and truth.

Self-Pity – A mindset focused on personal hardship without hope, often leading to emotional and spiritual stagnation.

Seeds of Faith – Small acts of belief and obedience that grow into deeper trust and greater purpose.

Spiritual Gifts – God-given abilities designed to serve and build up the Body of Christ.

Spiritual Growth – The deepening of faith, character, and relationship with God over time.

Strengths – God-given talents and abilities meant to be used for His glory and to serve others.

Surrender – Letting go of control and entrusting every aspect of life to God's will.

Testament – A declaration or evidence of God's faithfulness in one's life; often a personal story or witness.

Transformation – A profound and lasting change in character and behavior, driven by a relationship with God.

Trust in God – A continual reliance on God's promises, guidance, and goodness, even when outcomes are unclear.

Unstoppable – A mindset of holy confidence and purpose that persists through opposition, grounded in God's strength.

Wisdom – God-given insight for living rightly, often gained through experience, prayer, and Scripture.